CHALFORD
Oral History
SERIES

BLETCHLEY
voices

St Mary's bell ringers, early 1900s. (MH)

CHALFORD
Oral History
SERIES

BLETCHLEY
voices

Compiled by
Robert Cook

CHALFORD

First published 1998
Copyright © Robert Cook, 1998

Tempus Publishing Limited
The Mill, Brimscombe Port,
Stroud, Gloucestershire, GL5 2QG

ISBN 0 7524 1047 4

Typesetting and origination by
Tempus Publishing Limited
Printed in Great Britain by
Bailey Print, Dursley, Gloucestershire

The Bletchley contingent of the Buckinghamshire Battalion Home Guard, 1944. The old cricket
pavilion is in the background. (DRA)

CONTENTS

The Duchess of Abercorn locomotive and fireman on a foggy morning in December 1956, taking on water after missing the troughs at Castlethorpe. (BKBG)

KEY TO PICTURE CREDITS

DRA: Daphne R. Atkins.
DB: Dave Barrow. KB: Ken Barrow.
FB: Fred Bateman.
DFB: Donald Fraser Blane.
JB: Jack Blane. MB: Martin Blane.
JB: Jack Bromfield. BB: B. Brooksbank.
DC: Dennis Comerford.
RC: Robert Cook. MD: Midge Day.
RD: Rolly Doggett.
BKBG: B.K.B. Green.
MH: Margaret Hollis.

KJCJ: K.J.C. Jackson. RK: Reg Knapp.
EL: Edward Legg. GL: Glyn Lewis.
RL: Ray Lubbock. KM: Ken Mote.
NCE: *Northamptonshire Chronicle and Echo.*
JO: Judy Ounsworth. BP: Baden Powell.
BR: British Railways. CS: Colin Stacey.
JS: Jenny Stacey. RONS: Ron Staniford.
ROYS: Roy Stockham.
ST: Suzanne Tarpley. JW: Jim White.

INTRODUCTION

Everyone has their own impression of Bletchley, their own experiences. Times change and so do we. As Martin Blane observes in this collection, you get more of a kick out of life when you are young and you remember those times more intensely. For Ray Akins, however much the town has changed, the sun always shines on Bletchley because that is where he met his wife in the 1930s. For him the 'golden age' is always now.

Still, there is no harm in looking back through slightly rose-tinted glasses and there is no harm in casting a sceptical eye over all that is allegedly so much better for us today. The past should always inform the present and although people's memories are not always reliable, their impressions usually offer a very good insight into life.

Therefore, this is not a history book as such, but a collection of people's thoughts about the way Bletchley used to be and how it has changed. I hope that from each snapshot memory the book will build up a picture of Bletchley from the slow days of Emily Fennemore's childhood during the late nineteenth century to the tumultuous days of war and the beginnings of Milton Keynes, the new city development which seemed to threaten Bletchley's identity as a separate place. Of course, it is hard to say what that identity is or was.

The town could never have grown from a few thousand inhabitants in the 1920s to 37,395 at the 1991 census (not counting the rest of Milton Keynes on its borders) without lots of newcomers. These people came to inhabit the same place but their experiences are bound to vary. Newcomers have also brought tales and experiences from other places, but as ex-London fireman Frank McIntyre said, 'When we got up here we forgot about being Londoners or London firemen; we were all Bletchley.' They all make up the whole, and this book records some of their memories. These memories are clues to how people feel about the past more than matters of fact. There are always matters too personal to mention here, and as Ray Akins warned me, 'We'll only tell you about the ones we won.'

For me, Bletchley was the place where my father went to work driving brick lorries, which led to an accident and an early death. Though long ago, I still remember sneaky rides with him in those rattling old London Brick Company lorries. Sometimes he would take the whole family and our Alsatian dog out with him in those days of rapid post-war housing expansion which made the brickworks boom. That was all great fun, though father broke the company rules to allow it.

Bletchley was first and foremost a railway town. Not surprisingly, the railwaymen wove quite a community and established many customs, formal and informal. Inevitably, there is much to be said here about the railway tradition. For pioneering press photographer Ray Lubbock there were few rules. He boldly told me that when he started he knew nothing and learned as he went along. His employers, Ron Staniford and Harold Price, displayed an equal buccaneering spirit. As Ron

VIPs Aiden Crawley (centre left) and Aneurin Bevin (centre right) visiting Bletchley during the 1950 election campaign. (RL)

recalls, when he started the town's first newspaper his parents thought he was mad.

Ray thought big and optimistically about Bletchley when he wrote in the first edition of the *Bletchley Gazette*: 'Your own local newspaper at last! ... Do not confuse us when we talk of Bletchley. We mean it in its widest sense and seek to include in it surrounding smaller towns and villages, from Woburn to Winslow.' Not all would welcome such a broad definition and many were shocked by plans to expand the town in the 1950s, more so still ten years later when new plans for the London overspill threatened to engulf Bletchley in a new city development for 250,000 people. The *Northampton Chronicle and Echo* reported: 'Bletchley haunted by ghost of new city' and 'Bletchley Council in storm over new development'.

All that was over thirty years ago. As Ray Lubbock observes here, great plans were made to brighten up that part of Bletchley still known by its original name of Fenny Stratford, or 'Fenny'. Fenny was of reasonable size long before Bletchley. It was made prosperous by

George Temple Grenville, Marquess of Buckingham, when he backed the construction of the Grand Junction canal in 1792, which then suffered from the advent of the London-Birmingham railway in 1838.

I am grateful to all those who did so much to help me record as much as I have. The majority of the material used is from taped interviews. There is also a vital contribution from the late Emily Fennemore's memoirs. They were written in 1949 and date back to the nineteenth century. I am grateful to Mrs Fennemore's grandson, Ernest Allen, and her niece, Jean Raiders, for making this material available to me. Thanks are also due to Mrs Robert Maxwell for providing memories of campaigning with her husband for the North Bucks seat in parliament.

This collection would not be complete without the photographs and I am very much in debt to those kind enough to lend them. A key to the photographers is provided on p. 6. I would also like to thank Colin Stacey and Initial Photographics for their support.

Robert Cook

Sporting pupils at Bletchley Road School, late 1940s. (RL)

Simpson church. (BP)

Those Days

I was born in October 1908. As a boy I did a milk round for Makeham's at Sycamore Farm. I carried the milk in a two-gallon can with a hinged lid. There was a gill measure inside. I served the houses in Water Eaton. The round took about an hour. After taking the can back to the farm I walked to Leon School for class at nine o'clock.

Donald Fraser Bane

Over Stag Bridge, in those days made of iron, we came to The Gleve. Here lived a Mr and Mrs Stubbs, also big church workers. While they lived there they had a big fire in the stable and their favourite horse was burnt to death. On the other side of the road was Staple Hall, with a lot of farm buildings and lovely fruit gardens. As a child I used to go and help Mrs Adams pick fruit and used to take her butter round to a few special friends. Living with Mrs Adams was a minister named Mr Riddle.

Emily Fennemore
(the first of eight children born to Frank and Sarah Howard who were married at Simpson church in September 1872)

The cottage, 59 Mill Road, Water Eaton, where we lived, was basically two up, two down and until about 1950 had very few of the utility services we accept as normal these days. A tin bath in the scullery served for bathing. The toilet was at the bottom of the garden. I remember an old, black range in the kitchen which my mother used to black-lead regularly. She used a paraffin cooker in the scullery, on which she produced delicious meals. Her speciality

10

Water Eaton village, early 1900s. (MB)

was Victoria sponges, all light as a feather and second to none for taste. A small, triangular room was attached to the left of the cottage, and access could be gained from inside the cottage and through an external door in Mill Road. The room was used as a schoolroom in the early 1900s.

Daphne R. Atkins

A Billy Gayton Haircut

We used to have a barber's down Denmark Street, Billy Gayton. We used to say, 'Billy Gayton for pudding basin haircuts'. It cost two old pennies when you had one and afterwards you didn't have much hair left. But my father used to do ours and if it was lopsided he used to say, 'Oh well, boy, there's nothing a week won't put right.' But everyone recognized a Billy Gayton haircut.

Martin Blane

There was Burley's the barber in Fenny Stratford. It is reputed that Jack Johnson, the famous American boxer, had his hair cut there before the First World War, so my father told me.

Fred Bateman

Not Enough Room

My bedroom was very small, only room for one, but prettily papered. There was a single iron bedstead, two chairs and a dressing table.

Gwen Akins (née Burridge)

11

No more Billy Gayton haircuts, this is the modern style in Princes Way. (RC)

Ron King used to go up and down Bletchley Road in a four-wheeled chair with two handles to work a chain. The authorities wouldn't let him go to school after he woke up one morning and couldn't walk. First his mum, then his dad died. The boy had to go in a home by the time he was fourteen. He's been there ever since. There was no room in the school for him so he never learned much that way.

Jack Blane

Serious Men

My father was a farmer at Newton Longville. I went to school in the village until I was eleven. Then I went to Bletchley Road. The war had just started. I never really liked Bletchley Road. Mr Robinson from Stewkley took us on his bus. He was a serious man and we had to be well behaved. School teachers were strict. You daren't upset the headmaster, Mr Cook. He sometimes shouted. Just looking at him made you decide never to argue. The girls wore white blouses and gymslips.

Midge Day

Two Girls Beat Me!

I was born in 1913 at No. 4 Western Road. I was the only boy. All I can remember of the First World War was that my father was called up when I was about three. He was posted to Ireland to help keep the revolts down. I well remember news coming through of a troop ship being mined and going down at sea en route for Ireland. My mother was worried stiff until she found out that father wasn't on it.

I went to a little private school for the first year or two and then to Bletchley Road Boys'. In those days there wasn't comprehensive education. You had to pass the exam to get to the grammar school at Wolverton. I passed with the third highest mark in the county. Two girls beat me.

Ron Staniford

Housewifery as Well

Our school playground was opposite the recreation ground. Sometimes when we were at school we were allowed out into the recreation ground. The boys did gardening, we did cooking in a special domestic science room with quite a nice lady teacher. We did housewifery as well, learning to polish furniture. Sometimes when the governors came round we had to do a meal and serve it to the governors in the dining room.

Gwen Akins

On a warm, sunny spring day, to cycle up the hill from the Eight Bells was indeed a pleasure. Overhanging Lord Leon's wall were red and white laburnum and may bobs. On the left was a wide grass verge, a deep ditch and a hedge. The verge was rich with large patches of violets and across the field stood a row of large elms. The only sound was of rooks cawing away, busy building their nests. Only rarely we saw a car, more likely traffic was a horse

Sidney Clarke, farmer and milkman, at Newton Longville in the 1930s. He delivered to Bletchley when customers took their milk in jugs. (MD)

and cart. We were a group of girls on cycles, dressed in navy blue and gold, heading for Elmers Grammar School during the late 1920s. The school was for day and boarding pupils. Mr and Mrs Roberts had brought the school from Bletchley Road to Elmers.

Margaret Hollis (née Crane)

By thirteen years old I worked an early morning paper round for Mr Turner, the newsagent in Bletchley Road. Evenings and Saturdays I worked for Mr Staniford who sold wines and

From left to right Nesta Powell, Hope Still, Audrey Chester and Margaret Crane make a tennis foursome in St Martin's House, Elmers Grammar School, 1932-33. (MH)

spirits. I delivered orders.

Jack Blane

Very Keen on Face Powder

The boys' and girls' schools were separated. I took scones round the boys' school on a sieve, selling them for a halfpenny each. My boyfriend at the time was a pupil. Towards Christmas we did an opera or pantomime with the boys in their school. My boyfriend was there and instead of practising and doing things I ought to be doing, I was playing about with him. Then I felt very disgraced because I was called out for messing about and sent back to the girls' school. That was in or about 1928. I was born in 1916. I am and always have been a Methodist and this boy had to be one of the boys from the Sunday School. If we went carol singing with a group from the chapel it was nice because you could meet up with your pal and hold hands. I was romantic. I didn't feel girls were second class citizens, except for education. My father was one of the most loving. My mother was the one who controlled us. She'd been matron at an orphanage at Kempston. She was matronly and I had to do as I was told. On a Saturday I couldn't go out anywhere unless I'd polished the dining room chairs. One day I took my brother Donald, who was about one and a half, to Turner's paper shop. I'd got my cousin from Marston with me. I'd got to pay the papers for mum. I'd got some of my own money – I don't know where I'd got it from. It was an old sixpenny piece. At that time I was very keen to buy some face powder so we forgot all about Donald. We went to the chemist and bought the powder and came home. Mum said, 'Where's Donald?' 'Oh,' I said, 'Did I take him?' She said, 'Yes, you did.' I'd been gone about an hour. So we went back and Mr Turner said, 'Oh, Gwen, I knew that was your baby brother, he's been sitting out there in that pram as good as gold.' I can see him in my mind's eye now, a lovely little brown furry coat he'd got.

Gwen Akins

14

Bletchley bus station in recent years, with Robinson's school bus still going strong. (RC)

A Small Village Then

Bletchley was a village then really. There was only one place you could get a cup of drink, that was the Lantern Café. Sixpence for a cup of coffee and two coppers for some biscuits. It was on the left-hand side as you come down from Fenny near the old Co-op.

Ray Akins

Everybody thought I was going to marry Ron Staniford. He ran the *Gazette*. My mum was annoyed because all my brothers left the Methodist Church to go to the Baptists with Ron. I've only one brother left in England, he was the eldest and played Ron up. My other brothers emigrated to Australia.

Gwen Akins

Night shift men at the brickyard set wire cage traps on the edge of knot holes (pits from which the brick clay was extracted). They caught rats, then let them out on the canteen floor, chased them and killed them. When I was a boy starting at the brickworks, one of the old hands emptied his tea leaves on my head as he left the canteen so I tipped my whole mug over him. Served him right – I wasn't having that.

Jack Blane

In my early years, horsepower was just that. Cars, lorries and tractors were few in number. But horses were very much in use, pulling all sorts like milk floats loaded with churns and milk cans. They were even used in marshalling yards. Carters came from the villages collecting items for village folk. Rowland's the timber merchant used

A Sunday School Nativity scene in the Freeman Memorial Hall, early 1960s. (RL)

four large horses to haul massive tree trunks. All this real horsepower provided some very useful manure. It was usual to see people appear in the street with bucket and shovel. They either had sixth senses or good noses, but at least those sorts of traffic weren't harmful and the roses did well.

Our outdoor games changed with the seasons. We often played in the road quite safely. Motor vehicles were few and far between and we had ample time to avoid the horses and carts – their clip-clopping hooves gave early warning.

Martin Blane

There used to be two carriers come into town, Mr Capel from Loughton who always wore a smock frock, and Mrs Holton from Little Brickhill. She had a donkey cart. There was not much excitement in those days. I can remember the soldiers going through when they were changing places, and of course a German band. Sometimes an Italian would bring a dancing bear, then there was Joey Brandom, the organ grinder and lamplighter.

Emily Fennemore

We couldn't afford to keep the car after we got married as we needed the money to furnish the house. Freddy Cook drove a horse and cart at the brickyard before the war. There was a story up and down Newton Road that he'd trained a Derby winner. They never told me which one!

Jim White

Behind the scenes, coalman Josie Tarbox prepares his horses for the 1935 Jubilee pageant. (ST)

Own Entertainment

In the 1920s we often made our own entertainment. I founded the Busy Bees Concert Party, a sort of seaside show, end of pier type performance. They ran for five or six years, giving concerts around the villages. There were lots of people involved, actors, singers and electricians. We had our own portable floodlights, carting everything around in a little van. I remember getting to a little place called Botolph Claydon. We got out and discovered they'd only got oil lamps in the village hall so we had to perform by lamplight.

Ron Staniford

One-Horse Town

When we first came to Bletchley it was a one-horse town. The baker and the vegetable man came round on horse-drawn carts. I bought our house in Beechcroft Road new in 1939 but let it during the war. We had the pick of the road when these houses were going up in 1938 but we couldn't move in until 1945.

Reg Knapp

The Girl for Me

The night I decided Gwen Burridge was the girl for me was dark and we were walking arm in arm down Water Eaton – as befits a gentleman, with me walking on the outside. However, we

Producer Leslie Clare conducts a meeting of the Bletchco Players, reading parts for the hilarious production *Is Your Honeymoon Really Necessary?*, Easter 1967. (ROYS)

were on the wrong side of the road. I felt a sharp blow on my right shoulder and spun round into a dry ditch. I had been hit by a Morris 8 driven by an elderly lady who was much more upset than I was. Gwen rushed up and bent over, saying 'Are you hurt?' 'No.' Did she upbraid me for being on the wrong side of the road? No. To my surprise she whispered, 'Don't forget the insurance!' There and then I decided to propose as soon as possible!

Ray Akins

Old King George V

As a boy it was a Saturday ritual to call in Polly Howard's shop and get a halfpenny bag of sweets. Then it was twopence for the County cinema in Fenny High Street. Then it was called the 'Old King George V'. Twopence-halfpenny was our lot for the week, but it was all well spent. The cinema was renamed at the start of the war. Bill Betteridge kept it.

Fred Bateman

The County cinema was always known as the local flea pit. The 'Studio' was more upmarket.

Roy Stockham

Saturday Heroes

Bill Betteridge used to walk up and down in his cinema. There was no

Beechcroft Road during the 'Big Freeze' of 1963. (RK)

hanky panky. The cowboys used to have   them all shouting about at the screen,

The market in Aylesbury Street, Fenny Stratford, *c*. 1920. (MB)

The County cinema, High Street, Fenny Stratford, also known as 'The Palace' or 'The Old King George V', *c.* 1919. (RD)

hanky panky. The cowboys used to have them all shouting about at the screen, especially when someone was creeping round a rock: 'Look out, look out!' they'd start, and old Bill would call, 'Start shouting about and you're out.' If you were lucky you nipped in the balcony. You were made if you got up there. Cost about one and threepence normally. But if it was full up down below and one of your gang knew the usherette you might get up there. Then you could throw stuff like orange peel on people below. Those were the days of Ken Maynard, Buck Jones, Hopalong Cassidy and the Cisco Kid. They were our Saturday heroes.

Fred Bateman

Two ounces of sweets cost a penny, a gobster a farthing. Gobsters changed colour as you sucked. We got lucky bags with a black bean in. We bought bags of broken biscuits for a few coppers. We didn't get much pocket money, but twopence got us into the old County cinema down Watling Street. Saturday matinées were right noisy. We threw orange peel, watched Rin Tin Tin, Tom Mix, Harold Lloyd, Charlie Chaplin. Then there was the Pathé and Movietone news and bigger pictures like *Fu Man Chu* and the opium dens. That was for grown-ups though and got people very worked up. Cartoons were good. I remember *Felix the Cat*, he kept on walking.

Martin Blane

Hot Water

We lived at Brooklands Road. It was in the middle of a terrace of about sixteen. There was a continuous blue brick pathway along the rear of the terrace. We had a small living room kitchen which had a red and black tiled floor. The tiles were mostly covered with square patterned linoleum. There was a sofa under which boots were stored at night. The kitchen table was covered with a light coloured oil cloth. There was a coal-fired range with an oven on one side and a water boiler on the other, all recessed in an alcove. I do not remember the water boiler ever being used. A kettle was our usual source of water. The coal range was cleaned every Saturday and polished with brushes – there were a lot of brush factories in Bletchley. A coal man called each week with his horse and cart. Coal came in half-hundredweight or hundredweight hessian sacks. He carried them on his back.

Donald Fraser Blane

Hymns All Day

My grandfather Harry was a carrier. He wrote letters to people and looked after their welfare. Grandma and Grampy Burridge were some of the kindest people, though poor. I loved them. They had a big family and I remember having to wash outside in cold water even in winter. Grandma cooked lovely plain food. Grampy Burridge sat on his coal cart singing mainly hymns all day. He was very anti-Catholic.

Gwen Akins

Josie Tarbox and Scamp at home near the family's coal yard, Fenny Stratford, in 1934. Josie's daughter-in-law, Kathleen, said she washed the dog so much that he went this bright colour! (ST)

Patches on Our Clothes, but Never a Dull Moment

There was great excitement in the street when the sweep was coming – everybody up early. We couldn't light the fire so, being winter, we needed all our clothes on. The great moment for the children was when they went outside to see the brush come out of the top of the chimney pot.

Donald Fraser Blane

Puppeteers at Bletchley Road School, *c*. 1948. (RL)

Most kids had a patch in their shorts and thought nothing of it. We used to swim in Water Eaton millpond. The water was always moving. It was always moving and only four feet deep.

Martin Blane

Life for children wasn't dull, though it was simpler than today. Each child had to do certain chores in turn, such as sweeping the bricked yard, gathering food like dandelions and clover to feed the rabbits, which were kept in huts and killed for eating when grown. We kept chickens for eggs. We used a truck made from a grocer's sugar box to collect manure for the back garden. It meant getting up early in the morning and going along the roads most used by horses, shovelling up dung and bringing it home before we went to school.

Donald Fraser Blane

Navy Blue Knickers

As far as I remember we always wore our own clothes for school, sometimes a pinafore, and I remember button boots, black stockings and horrid thick nave blue knickers. Oh, they were itchy!

I liked school very much. I never went to grammar school. I ought to have done but I'd got four brothers. I was the oldest and my father thought I ought to be satisfied I'd get married. That broke my heart because I always wanted to be a teacher. I used to play the piano at school and got on well with all the teachers.

Gwen Akins

On Mondays we were usually allowed to sit at our classroom desks to eat our meal and then went into the playground until the bell sounded. Typical dress for boys would be long black woollen stockings secured with black garters above the knee, a grey flannel shirt and jacket. Always lace-up boots when young and perhaps a pair of shoes on Sunday after twelve years of age. The boots had to be polished with blacking which was sold in a tin and required some spit to soften it. Boys occasionally wore a cap. In summer they wore shorts and sometimes plimsolls. On Sundays a boy wore a suit if he had one for Sunday School. His collar would be celluloid, attached to the shirt with studs. Girls wore their best dresses.

Donald Fraser Blane

When the school doctor came he told mum that I was to have Parrish's Chemical Food, cod liver oil and malt. I hated it. I was thin and weedy. You'd never believe it now, would you?

Gwen Akins

I was later getting on than others because I had TB in the left leg bone. My brothers used to wheel me around in a push chair from three years old until I was six and could walk again. They took me birds' nesting and argued whose turn it was to push. None of them wanted to do it. When they got home my parents wanted to know where I was and my brothers got a flea in their ears. We had many a good laugh. Bletchley was very countrified then.

Martin Blane

Jolly hockey sticks! Bletchley ladies' team in the early 1930s. (BP)

I hardly ever had a doctor before the National Health Service came in. I remember having measles or chickenpox. I remember a doctor coming in. I suppose my parents had to pay.

Ron Staniford

We were brought up to be tough. There weren't no messing about, mate! Harrington used to play the organ in Fenny church and if I could escape from Sunday School I'd go and pump the organ. It was a pleasure to get out of Sunday School. We had lessons on religion and hymn-singing.

Jack Blane

Indigestion

My mother, Kathleen Southwell, married Edward Tarbox, a coal merchant's son. Their yard was near Fenny Stratford railway crossing gates. She was married at twenty-three and widowed by twenty-five. Edward died of peritonitis in around 1939, on Friday the thirteenth. He'd been going to the doctor, who said he'd got indigestion.

Suzanne Tarpley

Plus Twos and Lucky

I came to work at Bletchley brickworks in 1935 when there were three million unemployed. When I first went in the yard they said, 'Sorry, no vacancies'. I got my job through a Chief

Gone fishing: Reg Sfakianos and William Southwell enjoy a bit of nature by the canal near Fenny Stratford, *c.* 1935. (ST)

Tarbox coal merchants join the motor age, late 1920s. (ST)

Beechcroft Road coronation celebrations, 1953. (RK)

Engineer who was with me in the merchant navy. It was pretty lonely at sea and this engineer had retired to Leighton Buzzard. I was living in London, where I was staying with my sister, and he sent me a telegram. He'd seen this job advertised. There was some consternation when I arrived for interview wearing plus twos. I remember the works manager saying, 'I can't imagine him packing up the sea to come here for a quarter of the wage.' I'd been in Dr Barnardo's Homes from 1911 to 1923 and then naval school.

Reg Knapp

Hand-made Bikes but No Changing Gear

You were lucky if you had a push bike, most kids learnt on an old one. I got my first when I was fourteen. There was quite a cycling group in the town. They went all over the place, even down to Abertillery in Wales. We usually bought our bikes from one of the Luton Wheelers, Charlie Coles. He owned a cycle shop in Dunstable. Quite a character he was. My brother and me went on holiday with him to the south of France just before war broke out so we had quite a holiday because everything was cheap – not many people were going. We had hotels nearly to ourselves, and first class service. None of our bikes had gear changers. We went all the way to Wales with a 72, that's a fairly high gear. In winter we'd change the back sprocket to what we called a 54. Being a lower gear you could pedal faster to keep warm. You had to be careful going down hill with a fixed wheel but you were all right if you kept a steady rhythm. We got to Sherwood Forest in a day. The friend I went with had relatives at Beeston, where we stayed before going on over the hills from Buxton to Glossop. We didn't have to worry about roads plagued with traffic. They were quiet. They were the best years of our life – we could ride two abreast and chat away. There were some accidents though. Dick Goodman and his younger brother, 'Webby', were good. 'Webby' was out with my brother one Sunday morning. They'd been to a time trial meeting and were on their way home when he was knocked off and killed.

That was our youth. You get more out of life when you're young. They were our best days, particularly the cycling, taking your lunch with you, calling at a pub for a bottle of beer.

Martin Blane

A London Hotel

My aunt, Eleanor Southwell, went as a receptionist to a London hotel where she met Baron Sfakianos and were soon to marry. Their son went to Sandhurst and became a major.

My grandmother was a cook in service. She had to come home to look after Mrs Southwell who died shortly after childbirth. Mr Southwell didn't wait long to remarry. Women did as they were told. Mr Southwell married Ellen Watley. They had four children; one died. The horses reared up on the day of the funeral and they had to bring the coffin back. This was seen as a bad omen, meaning another death. Four months later Mr Southwell died and another baby was born. Mrs Southwell married Robert Chappell which her

It's a long way back to Bletchley! Martin Blane takes a rest from pedalling, having reached as far as Sherwood Forest in less than a day in around 1935. (MB)

boys resented, I think. They went off to sea. Bill Southwell went on minesweepers and I believe he won a medal.

Suzanne Tarpley

Turnips and Half a Banana

My dad was a very good gardener and had an allotment. He grew all these lovely turnips and potatoes. One thing I had to do, and I was a bit shy, was to go round Leon Avenue knocking on doors asking if people wanted to buy

Back to nature as weeds take over the redundant Bletchley brickworks in 1991. (RC)

them. I can't see children doing that these days. But my father being a guard on the railway didn't earn all that much to keep five children. There wasn't all that much money about. According to other people we were middle class, though we had to have only half a banana or cake for tea. We couldn't have a whole one. If we had a birthday party we were delighted to have jelly and blancmange, that was a highlight of the day.

Gwen Akins

Tradition and Change

My grandmother was Lizzie Webster, the eldest of twelve children, who married Charlie Goss of the well known Water Eaton family in 1898. My father,

Arthur Goss, was born in 1907, one of eight children. The Websters came originally from Leighton Buzzard where the first four children were born between 1873 and 1878. After moving to Duncombe Street, Bletchley, the remaining eight children were born between 1880 and 1894. Today there are many descendants of the Websters living and working on Vancouver Island, maintaining links with others in Newton Longville and Northampton.

Daphne R. Atkins

My father, Arthur Crane, rang the bells at St Mary's church from the age of fourteen until a week before he died aged seventy-five.

Margaret Hollis

St Mary's bell ringers between 1947 and 1955. From left to right: P. Daniels, Walter Sear, Joseph Marks, Arthur Crane, Harry Sear, Roger Cadamy. (MH)

Hands was a shortish, thickset man. One time he ran a pub on Buckingham Road, near the Methodist chapel. They also had a garage off the old station drive. People apart from doctors, professionals and aristocracy didn't have cars, so Hands ran a taxi service.

Martin Blane

Miss Meredith worked in the railway station buffet for years. We used the Temperance Tea Rooms. Most of us had shares in it. It was well patronized by railwaymen. You'd go across for your tea for threehalfpence or twopence. There was two or three regular ladies in there.

Fred Bateman

The Co-op was run by a committee. Bob Blane finished up as secretary of the Co-op and my friend Rose married him. I was bridesmaid for Rose's wedding. Bob was one of the best.

Gwen Akins

Most men had their hair cut at Richardson's on the corner of Queensway and Osborne Street, where most of the gossip would be about railway activities.

Donald Fraser Blane

To get on the railway you had to have two sponsors. Two Paceys sponsored me. One was Frank, an engine driver who lived opposite. The other was the ironmonger from where my parents bought a lot of furniture. Once you'd been one of his customers

Miss Meredith behind the station's buffet counter, October 1951. (BR)

he knew who you were. He said, 'You'll be a good boy, you won't let me down?' I said, 'No, Mr Pacey.' My father was a fireman so I was halfway there.

Fred Bateman

Respect for the Law

Inspector Calloway was police chief for many years and Sir Edward Duncombe was Chief Magistrate. Mr Hedley Clarke was the general factotum. He owned Bletchley Road Post Office and Labour Exchange. He organized the roasting of an ox in Leon recreation ground to celebrate VE Day, to which all inhabitants were invited.

Donald Fraser Blane

We had a police station at Fenny but not an awful lot of crime. In those days if you got caught biking without a light you could be fined. That's looked on as trivial now, but then there weren't the cars so it was less dangerous.

You'd be worried if a policeman caught you scrumping and said he'd tell your parents. It was enough to make you turn tail and run. You had respect for the law and didn't want to bring disgrace on

Pollard's ironmongers, formerly Pacey's, in Aylesbury Street. (RC)

your family. We were a big family – I was youngest of eight.

Martin Blane

Grated Soap Like Cheese

Those days you boiled water in a copper and grated up the soap like cheese. Someone had to get up early to light the fire under it. There were various gadgets to assist you washing. There was a washboard, the sort of thing that became popular with skiffle music groups in the fifties, and a dosher, or at least that's what we called it. The thing had holes in to let the water through and you doshed it up and down in the washing, a bit like the washing machines do these days.

As children we all had our jobs. I would clean potatoes, light the fire every day. That's the only way of coping, just like the old woman who lived in a shoe. We were better off for that. As the others left to start work, I had more to do.

They were all long livers on my father's side. His sister reached 103 and my mother was ninety-two when she died. She was originally a schoolteacher. She encouraged all of us.

Martin Blane

Out to Work

Only one of my brothers went to grammar school. He was the only one they could afford to go. All the rest of us left at fourteen. Before I left school I did a paper round. Then I was apprenticed in shoe making and repairing. But I didn't go back after the

31

VE Day celebrations, Leon Rec. (RONS)

RAF and war service.

Martin Blane

My brother went to grammar school and became an architect. Parents couldn't afford for all their children to go. I left school at fourteen, but I was interested in technical drawing and studied at evening school. I did German as well but then the war came and changed everything.

Fred Bateman

We push-biked to work. Most had bikes. A few had motor bikes. Folks were poor then. It took half an hour from Woburn to Bletchley brickworks. I got one shilling and fourpence halfpenny an hour. You had to save a penny where you could. I averaged just over £3 a week and that was good wages.

Bubbles Field

Prehistoric Animals

They found prehistoric animal bones in the knot holes (brick clay pits). They put some of these on display in the office when I first joined. One day in 1936 the works manager brought in a bowl containing gold coins and some dog bones. Another day he came in with a big rock. You could make out this squashed fish, its eyes and skeleton. They reckoned it was fifteen million years old.

Reg Knapp

Jimmy Dig Deeper

I've seen old 'Jimmy Dig Deeper' come out of the kilns where he'd been sleeping, on a cold and frosty morning in the brickyard. The brook running through the yard was frozen in those winter months. He'd only have his old trousers on. He'd go and smash the ice, get his old soap out and have a good wash down. One night he came back from the pub, he'd been shopping as well. He was so drunk he ate the soap for supper and tried washing with the cheese!

Bubbles Field

Nicknames

There was an advert for Pears soap about when I was a boy. It showed a curly-haired little boy blowing bubbles. I'd been playing in the yard with some other littl'uns. Then we came in our farmhouse for tea. One of the little girls sat down and looked at me and said, 'There's Bubbles!' and the name stuck.

Bubbles Field

My nickname was 'Brusher' for obvious reasons! Cyril Flexney, foreman on the loading dock at the brickworks was called 'Flannel Foot' or 'Windmill Foot' because he walked with his feet at ten to two. They reckoned that when he left the office on the narrow dock he had to go right to the end to turn round!

Jack Bromfield

Bubbles Field, nicknamed after the Pears soap boy. (RC)

Healthy Times

My dad, Sidney Clark, delivered the milk to Mr Keep in Park Street and everybody around Newton Longville, measuring it out in jugs. It was lovely growing up in Newton. Everybody used to help each other. We played hopscotch, rounders, marbles and skipping with a long rope stretched across the road. We'd jump out of the way if we heard a car coming but there weren't many. There was a regular baker's van from the Co-op.

Midge Day

Cyril Flexney supervises snow clearance at the entrance to the Newton Road brick works, January 1963. (RK)

There was only one school when I started, Leon in Bletchley Road. Everybody went there. They bussed pupils in from Stoke Hammond, Shenley, Loughton, Simpson, Wavendon and Newton Longville. We were a fairly healthy family. My parents paid into the National Deposit Friendly Society, monthly at St Martin's Hall, until the National Health Service came in after the war. There was a scarlet fever outbreak in 1946 and the house had to be fumigated. There was an isolation hospital on the way out to Linslade. My brother went there. When he came back he had a banana! I was named after Dr Roland Reynolds. He

died quite young. In my youth we went to Dr Maddison and during the war, to the elderly Dr Dorothy Lovekin. Dr Reynolds had a surgery at the corner of Brooklands Road. Dr Maddison took over from Dr Reynolds who was called up during the war. The doctor wore tweeds and thick brown stockings.

Rolly Doggett

Social Workers

Delivery roundsmen were the social workers. If someone wasn't well they'd deliver a note. They'd help take messages to people, even your grocery order. We had a butcher, baker and blacksmith in the village and there used to be a packman, he had goods packed on his bike. He showed you this and that and he'd get it for you. I remember his asking mother if she wanted razor blades for the boy and she said, 'No, he doesn't smoke!', not thinking.

Baden Powell

Lovely Roast Dinners

A lot of people in Fenny went to Benford's. He was a noted poultry man, always had a lot of game hanging there. He was a good butcher.

Fred Bateman

We always had a roast dinner. The Co-op butcher was next to the Fenny Stratford Co-op. Mum always managed to buy a lovely joint of beef, better than we have today because it

Benford family butchers, Simpson Road, c. 1935. (GL)

was big. We were lucky because we had a Rayburn and she always used to cook lovely roast dinners. Not only did she teach me to cook – and I've taught my two daughters – but my four brothers as well. Whenever I had any new cakes for sale in the Co-op confectionery department, like chocolate fudge, I'd buy it, take it home and analyse it with one of my brothers. We'd keep on making it until we got it right. We were lucky we had a mother who would let us mess about.

Co-op delivery vans and other bakers came to me for loads. They came in through the front door and at the back

of the counter were rows of boxes of toffees, coconut ice and all that sort of stuff. I had a window so that if I was packing out the back I could look into the shop. Every time this particular baker, Bill, called, he'd put his hand in those toffees. He had a liking for them. I worked on a leakage system – the hardest system you could work on. You were only allowed so much leakage a year. One day I said to Bill, 'Let's see how much those toffees weigh that you've got in your pocket.' He couldn't do any other. Do you know, his hand held over a quarter of a pound of toffees every time he took them and that

Memorial service at Cardington for the victims of the R101 airship disaster, November 1930. (MH)

showed up in my leakage because he came in every day.

Gwen Akins

Prize Window Display

I did my courting putting displays in the confectionery shop window at the Co-op instead of walking down leafy lanes. Gwen won a prize for the best window display. Then I used to go and help her dismantle them and we used to throw loaves at each other when the blinds were down.

Ray Akins

Easter Rats

The bakery was at the back of my shop but then they moved up to Albert Street. There was all this empty bakehouse with the big ovens at the bottom. Well, I used to use the great big baking tables to put the orders on for Winslow, Tingewick and all around. One Easter I'd got them all out lovely. Easter eggs, beautiful. Well, one spring morning one of the orders had completely gone. We knew there hadn't been a burglar; there were no signs of doors and windows interfered with and they'd have taken the lot. It was just this one order. Nobody ever knew until they decided to take down the old bakery and build a garage. They dismantled the ovens and found the

Easter eggs intact. They found that rats from the cattle market had come in. One rat would lie on its back with an egg on its belly and another would pull it by the tail.

Gwen Akins

Last Respects

In November 1930 the Royal Antedeluvian Order of Buffaloes (the Buffs) from all over England went to Cardington Royal Airship Works about twenty miles away. It was a Sunday. They paid their last respects to the victims of the R101 airship disaster. The airship used to be tested over the Bletchley area, Cardington not being far away. Many people heard it groaning away low in the sky above them, massive thing, like a big cigar case. Half the victims of the crash in France had been Buffs and their brethren wanted to make a special tribute. The service was conducted by Revd F.W. Bennitt from Bletchley and Bletchley's St Mary's church choir led the singing. I was among them. Among the hymns we sang were 'Through the night of doubt and sorrow' and 'Eternal Father, strong to save'.

Margaret Hollis

CHAPTER 2
Railway times

Engine no. 44869 on Bletchley flyover, 27 October 1964. (CS)

Oh, To Be an Engine Driver!

When I was a boy, I wanted to be an engine driver. I knew a lot more about engines than a good many working on the footplate. My dad wouldn't let me. He was a fitter in the engine sheds. He didn't want me having the muck and the dirt my mother would have to cope with. There was no laundry service in those days. He said, 'You can go onto the railway if you go into the traffic department.' So I started up there. I'd been at work a year when I got a job as a train reporting boy in the telegraph office. All trains had to be reported and messages carried along the line so people in control knew where the trains were. It wasn't Morse as such. We used a double plate sounder with two little hammers. You could screw the hammers around the heads. One went clunk, the other went click. It was left or right rather than long or short. They had a big radio station in the old goods yard during the war in case a bomb dropped on the land lines.

Jack Bromfield

'Let the Old Bugger Lay in!'

They had call-up boys to get the train crews up in the night, that was how they started out working their way up to be drivers. My dad was a driver. I remember him saying about lying awake in the early hours in his bed at Brooklands Road and hearing the call-up boys out in the street saying they couldn't remember whether it was No. 14 or 16. So one of them said, 'Well let's leave the old bugger in bed.' They copped it: when he got in, he reported them!

Jack Blane

When I first started calling up it was 1937. I was fourteen. The lights used to go out at midnight. There were two or three drivers used to live up Tattenhoe Lane. That was the wildest of the wild in those days. There were no estates. Fourteen years of age, pedalling up there on a bicycle, I used to be as frightened as old Harry. When you went up by Captain Whiteley's place it was all trees and then a fence. There were no houses and the wind would whistle across through the trees. You'd think, 'Who's that?' The only consolation was there were two or three policemen about. Once they got to know you you were all right.

Fred Bateman

Old Nally Tarbox

As a boy going to work in the railway telegraph office I'd walk up the old station approach. I remember I used to see old Nally Tarbox at six in the morning. He worked in the loco sheds and cycled in at about four miles a fortnight! He used to say, 'Good morning, young man, 6-4 to field, is this the road to Paradise?' He'd always say something like that. One morning he was walking with his bike. I said, 'Got a puncture?' 'No. Never had time to get on,' he replied, quick as lightning.

Jack Bromfield

Bletchley roofless loco 58887, September 1953. (BKBG)

Clean Trousers for Me

I got frightened out of my wits one night going up Albert Street to call up driver Fred Eastaff. His wife was very ill. He didn't want me to knock the knocker. It was about two in the morning. He was standing at the gate and it was pitch black. I'd only got the old boneshaker with an oil lamp on it that they used to give you. He was standing at the gate and when I stopped he stepped out from the dark and put his hand on the handlebars. I thought, 'Oh no! Clean trousers for me!'

Fred Bateman

A Good Old Yarn with Mr King

Drivers had a round tin with their number on it where their pay was put. I'd go down a Friday if dad was booked off and collect it from the sheds. Then I'd go and watch Bill King the blacksmith. He had a lot of work to do because the railways used heavy horses for shunting and he made frames for firing the locos. I used to draw up a stool by the blacksmith's fire. Quite a few men used to wander in for a chat in the cold weather. I suppose they were more careful talking while I was there. The blokes liked a good old yarn, sport or anything, taking the mickey. Of course all those engine sheds have

Inside Bletchley loco sheds, late 1940s. (BR)

gone long ago. I got on well with Bill King. He knew my dad and my brother. Everyone knew everyone else in town, you felt part of a community.

Martin Blane

Spinner Atkins

There was always some Jack the Lads about in those days. There was a Bletchley driver called Ernie 'Spinner' Atkins and there was an old boy, Fred Butterfield, who used to book the men on and off at a window. The poor old boy was a bit blind and a bit cantankerous but they used to pull his leg. This here Spinner Atkins used to put on a false moustache, pull his hat down and he used to say to Fred: 'Give us the foreign sheet [the list of drivers from other stations booked off for rest periods at Bletchley depot].' If the 'foreign' men booked off, they went over to accommodation under the water tank outside the station. There were three or four bedrooms there. The call boy looked after them. There was a set of men in there for eight hours' rest, booked off. In the morning they'd work a train back to their own station. Anyway, Spinner would, in his disguise, go up to Fred's window, using his native broad Nottinghamshire accent, and say something like, 'Giz this er ur sheet – set of er Tanko men bookin' off.' 'Oh alright, mate,' he'd say and put the sheet out of the window. Then when the foreman came out there was no-one there. He'd say to old Fred, 'What the 'ell yer talkin' about, Tanko men? There's no bugger 'ere.' Old Spinner had had him, hat down and all that.

Fred Bateman

The canal at Fenny Stratford, c. 1900. (JO)

One Foggy Night

I trained to be a signalman. The main line was very busy but on the branches it was like Will Hey's *Ghost Train* film. When I was at Fenny Stratford signal box the police station was opposite. The old sergeant liked tea and used to come over for some of mine. He was with me one foggy night. The distant signal was right up by Bow Brickhill crossing. I had to get it off in good time when a heavy brick train was coming up from Forders. If it stopped they'd need an extra engine to get it going again. I had to open the gates before the signal would go off, so I started turning the wheel. It got so far and then 'thump', it wouldn't go. I tried this a few times. Then I said to the sergeant that we'd better go down and have a look. Got down, there were these horses and donkeys escaped from a field by the line. I think they were animals used to carry children at the seaside during summer. We drove them into Rowland's wood yard. I don't know what they thought next day.

Jack Bromfield

Big End Corks

All those signal boxes were connected by an open telephone line. If one box answered the phone all the others would hear and lift their receiver. They should only have answered if they heard their code, but there was all sorts of gossip and they all liked to listen in. I can remember trying to get a message down to Swanbourne sidings and the signal was that weak. I said there must have been a lot of folk listening in that night. We used these

View from Fenny Stratford signal box, Simpson Road, *c.* 1947. (JB)

big corks to seal the oil in the steam engines' big end bearings, and we carried spares. Signalmen would get some off us and use them to plug the voice end of their box phones so no-one knew they were listening.

Fred Bateman

Never Two Days the Same

I was living in Bletchley in 1937. I got a job as a porter for a while on the LMS railway. The work was never two days the same – delivering goods in the area by dray. There were about three brush factories in town – the main one was Cook's. I collected brushes for distribution by rail.

Ray Akins

Lap-top Soup

The London-Liverpool Express was nearing Leighton Buzzard. I received the appropriate bell code from signalman Frank Burgoyne at Chelmscote bridge box (four rings). I pulled off the down fast home and distant signals. They were still operated by the original levers even though they were colour light signals. The lever frame was LNWR pattern. About six inches had been cut off the hand hold at the top of the lever (in my opinion, making it unbalanced). When the Liverpool came into sight beyond Chadwell bridge, I reversed the distant signal, turned round to send 'train entering section' to Bletchley No. 1 box and caught my backside on the stirrup of the home signal lever which flew back into the frame, setting the signal to danger. I grabbed the green flag and

43

stuck it out of the window but it was too late. The driver had already slammed the brakes on. The diners on the train ended up with having lap-top soup. I will leave you to guess what happened to Bromfield.

Jack Bromfield

The Killer

I was a plate layer and I suppose I was lucky to survive my accident on the Buckingham branch during the 1940s. Because of my injury I was transferred to flagging duties in the Bletchley area. I remember the old Caledonian Express. We used to call it 'the Killer'. I saw two men and a ganger working as it came along. I shouted but it was too late.

Bob North

A Tender Age

It all began one misty morning in November 1937 when at the tender age of fourteen years I was told to report to the running shift foreman at Bletchley at six o'clock in the morning to become a callboy. There were about 300 footplate men at the depot and 150 guards. All men signing on duty between midnight and seven o'clock had to be called or knocked up. Two of us lads were well employed doing this.

Fred Bateman

I worked on the station during the war. It was very sad seeing coffins being loaded onto trains. They were for young servicemen killed in training exercises at local airfields.

Mavis Dyson

Serving with the Home Guard during the war I remember guarding the signal box at Denbigh Bridge with a First World War rifle.

Baden Powell

Some of the older drivers and some guards could be miserable old sods. If they came ten minutes late they always blamed the callboy, when they'd probably rolled over and had another five minutes. One of the old callboys, Fred Harris, ended up as a driver on the Newport branch. He was a big, tall, gangly sort of kid. He used to wear big hobnailed boots. He went up the path to call one old driver who'd come rushing down thinking there was a horse loose on the path. Sound carries when all else is quiet.

Fred Bateman

Early Potatoes

Good Friday was the great day. You always reckoned to get your early potatoes in. The oldest allotments were off Water Eaton Road. Nearly all the railway men had a plot. Years later that was developed.

Martin Blane

Denbigh Bridge over the A5 (Watling Street) in 1954. Baden Powell recalls defending this signal box with his Home Guard platoon using a First World War rifle. (KB)

Fresh from the Garden

Every Sunday morning we had a lovely fry-up of mushrooms. Dad and his mates used to stop their goods train, get off and load a wicker basket with mushrooms. We didn't go short in the war because dad used to go booking off. He had a wicker basket with a lid to take fresh stuff from the garden. He'd take it on his train to London, book off and come back with things like salmon. We were well off.

Gwen Atkins

Quiet – Dad's in Bed

Most I remember about dad's work was him being on shift work all the time: 'Keep quiet, dad's in bed.' I can remember people coming out and knocking the door because they were thin on the ground for drivers, knocking him up in the early hours for work. Dad would come home about tea time, have his tea reheated. We'd had ours and his was left on the stove. I can't remember much more about railway life.

Jenny Stacey (née White)

All Honourable!

They used to have pigeon specials on the railways. These carried pigeons in baskets. They released them at various stations. They used to come from Cambridge and there was usually an envelope in the basket with a two-bob bit for the fellow who let them out. It was all honourable. No-one else would pinch it.

Fred Bateman

A class 9F loco hauling freight just outside Bletchley on the Oxford branch, *c.* 1960. (CS)

I went home from work one day, you could cut the atmosphere in the sitting room with a knife. My brother, Len, and my father just sat there glaring at each other. It was a while before I found out what was going on. My dad was a fitter at the engine sheds. Len was his mate, nicknamed 'Speedy'. Dad had hit his thumb with a hammer and thrown the tool halfway up the shed in a moment of pain and temper. Then he said to Len, 'Go and fetch it.' Len had a bit of a stutter in those days, and he said, 'You ttthrew the bbbloody tthing, you gggo and fetch it.' Dad chased him right out of the shed and up to the water tower, but of course he ran out of steam first.

Jack Bromfield

Post Office

I first came to the area during my wartime army days. I spent a lot of my working life at the Post Office. I went there in 1947. They were a happy crowd. There were three shifts, the early town walk, the early rural and the late rural. I started on £4 a week. Inspector Blake was the boss and Wilson was postmaster. On nights you had to meet the paper train. We sorted and despatched the mail. The bags were hung from the platform in leather pouches. The mail coaches had a net and scooped them off in a split second.

Cyril Freeman

Temperance Tea Rooms

We used to have some high jinks in our old tea cabin at night.

Releasing homing pigeons on Easter Monday 1955. (KB)

Someone would end up climbing onto the chimney and putting a bag over it. That would sort them out. We had an open fire.

Another trick they had involved the big tea urn. It held about four gallons of water and old Sammy Sanders had to have it boiling for two o'clock in the morning when they all went down to dinner. You'd be just going to make the tea, the big old cast iron kettle boiling away on the fire, and someone would drop an onion in. We had a good old fire. Camden coal we used; it came from Grimethorpe though.

Fred Bateman

Collision

I heard all about the collision on Bletchley station. It happened at the start of the war. I was in the army and heard it on the camp radio. I knew my fiancée Annie Budd would be arriving at the station about that time. It was a while before I knew she was safe.

Cyril Freeman

Old Irving Butler lost his life in that crash. There was an old Bletchley driver on that leading engine, a fellow named Harold. They missed the signals up at the sidings. The shunting engine was putting a coach on the back of one of the down Scottish trains. I believe there was a carriage shunter in between the engine and the vehicle uncoupling. I think his name was Clements. There were about four killed.

Fred Bateman

The approach to the station, *c.* 1900, showing the old post office building on the left. (DC)

Like a Bottle of Fizz!

Frank Burridge ended his days as foreman at Swanbourne sidings. Three or four established guards went. He was a nice, quiet fellow. His temperament was very placid. As a lad I used to go to the Wesleyan school. Frank used to go there when he was off. He'd do his job and you'd never hear him shouting about. If something went wrong he kept his equilibrium. He didn't go up in the air like a bottle of fizz, like some of them.

Fred Bateman

Dingy, *with Gas Lights*

When I first started firing at the beginning of the war there was a driver, Sammy Sanders. He'd failed his eyesight test for the main line. They gave him a job at Bletchley. He took lodgings and went home every weekend. He had to prepare engines, oiling them. He wasn't allowed on the main line. He got an hour an engine, eight a shift. Sammy assumed the status of being in charge of the canteen and tea fund. About three in the morning the men would come in, including Arnold Bromfield and the fitters. They'd start winding Arnold up. He'd go up like a bottle of fizz. I said, 'Let's have a quiet night,' but it would end up with someone putting a bag over the chimney and smoking them out. A horrible place it was – dingy, with gas lights. So the next day I'd come in and say again, 'Let's have a quiet night, please.' But it was half an hour of Bedlam, especially when old Bromfield was on. But he wasn't the only one, there were others who only wanted their fuse lighting.

Fred Bateman

The City of Liverpool on shed, now ready for the road after repairs, mid-1950s. (KJCJ)

A Duchess or a Princess

One of my most precious moments was on the Lakes Express. We used to have a job every Saturday down to Crewe and come back with the Lakes. You'd book off at Crewe, take your own tea and sugar, put an egg in. You'd have the eggs and bacon when you got up in the morning.

We used to have a Duchess or a Princess class loco on the Lakes, pulling seventeen coaches. We'd come up there, sitting in the seat, damn great long boiler in front, arms folded and hear her stomping away. The driver was busy and you'd think it's his turn now. The driver was captain of the ship but you had an understanding, you worked together, you might as well get on, you'd got to work together all day long. Some were a bit stroppy, you had to respect their rank. As a fireman you climbed on and cleaned the front of the boiler. Fred West would draw a line down the cab and only let you clean your side.

Controllers only spoke to drivers, not firemen. At Oxford old 'Bronco', the foreman, would say, 'You've got to have a forty-three, are you all right, driver?

49

Fred Bateman, the fireman on *Nobby Newport*, early 1950s. (FB)

Will you take her?' 'Yeh, ha, ha, as long as she's got wheels on.' But drivers wouldn't lead you astray. I remember Ern Hillesden on the shunter. He'd got two sons of his own firing, a nice little old boy from Oxford. He'd say, 'You wanna do this, my boy? You wanna do that?' I remember oiling the engine in the morning – the fireman always went underneath to oil the big ends. Ern would look through the frame to see that you were doing it. 'I'm much obliged, much obliged,' he'd say. He appreciated what you'd done.

Railways were a community. I think being in the sheds 'bar boying' you got used to engines and their ways. You needed a mechanical aptitude. As bar boys we used to tinker about the shed,

sitting in engines, pretending we were driving them.

There was nothing like old steam engines. Scooping up water on the run was a precision exercise. We used to come from Crewe with the Lakes Express, fill up just outside Crewe, then three more scoops before London. Bushey was the last one. You wanted scoops at all of them on those big engines. You could pick up 3,000 gallons in one scoop over about one and a half miles. Hademoor troughs were very difficult because there was a crossing just clear of them. Your scoop, or dip as we called it, was a galvanized pan under the tender. You'd be doing sixty-five to eighty miles an hour and wind this scoop down. As soon as it went in you eased off a bit. You'd see the gauge in the tender go up to about 4,000 gallons as quick as anything, straight up if you were going fast. On an express they only skimmed it. Scoops had to be replaced periodically as they'd sometimes get stuck.

Sometimes I drove old *Nobby Newport* on the short branch from Wolverton, where the railway works are, to Newport Pagnell. We used to go down in the morning, ten o'clock from Wolverton, and come back at one. When we got relief they'd bring us home in a bus, carrying the bean sticks we'd cut from the hedge along by Blackhorse bridge. All sorts of antics we got up to. We had a bit of spare time, we didn't need too long for shunting about in Newport yard. It was a four-mile run, mostly workmen for passengers. They used to go home to dinner. But by the time they'd walked to the station they could have caught a bus.

A Black 5 loco with parcels train passing Whiteley Crescent, late 1950s. (DB)

I remember one time on old *Nobby*: we'd have been up since four in the morning, it was a frosty old day so we left the steam heater on while we sat in Newport station, then we climbed into the carriage next to the engine and had our meal. It was so cosy we fell asleep. When we woke up, the fire was out in the engine and it was nearly time to take the men back to work. Ken West was my fireman guard and the pair of us had to go ripping up lineside fencing to get it started again. We'd still got 60 lbs of steam pressure so we knew there was a chance. We needed 120 lbs pressure to blow the vacuum. Still we were lucky to get going. The men were only half an hour late getting back to work. Another time was when the platelayers were working Sunday, which was very rare. Platelayer Ernie Clare asked me for this particular Sunday, whether I could drop him off a knob of coal at their cabin near Blackhorse bridge. They called Ernie the Red Lion ganger on account of his favourite pub. George Judge, my driver, said, 'You're gonna take one of them great lumps off the bunker which'll save you cracking it up.' So I rolled this lump off as we approached being in line with the cabin. That rolled off almost square with it, with a great cloud of dust as it bombed down the bank and through the cabin door, letting up another cloud of dust. Old Judge said afterwards, 'You've done it, you've wrecked the door, broke the stove and knocked it off its moorings!'

Fred Bateman

Smell and Smuts

Living in Beechcroft Road, we were near the Oxford branch line. When we had steam trains coming up from

Driver Fred Bateman prepares to board a class 8F loco at Swanbourne sidings, *c.* 1960. (FB)

Northampton. We had five, numbers 10201 to 10205 and then two LMS ones, 10000 and 10001. That was the first experience we had. To sit in an armchair was quite a novelty. We had to go to Derby for a conversion course on each class. I had my original basic training for diesels and then about nine conversions.

Fred Bateman

Swanbourne Sidings

We used to go down to Quainton Road. That was the exchange siding for Calvert. We used to pick up those big forty-tonners loaded with bricks. They used to come into Swanbourne sidings from Sandy at 5.45 a.m. on the front of a coal train – anthracite in from the Western Region bound for heating greenhouses in East Anglia's horticultural district. We used to take four or five of these big forty-tonners on the front of the train. They were a big help for your braking. When they got to Sandy, the Eastern Region took them over and raffled them off to various places in East Anglia. There was a big advantage in that the Oxford to Cambridge branch across country crossed so many main lines. It should never have closed. It wasn't Dr Beeching's idea or intention.

Fred Bateman

Bletchley a south wind would blow the smell and smuts across. No good at all if you were trying to paint the house. The half past one up from Bletchley was almost legendary. It shook all the houses. Where the roof joined the brick they all cracked. They were dirty great big engines with six-foot wheels.

Ray Lubbock

Armchair Drivers

The diesels at Bletchley were originally Southern Region. We used them on residential services up to

A Ghastly Mistake

I have been convinced all along that the Ministry of Transport and British

Railways have made a ghastly mistake. Bus operators can only provide a service on the Oxford-Cambridge route at the expense of providing an even worse service on other routes in the area.

Robert Maxwell, MP for Bletchley

Tough Guys

Discipline started to become an issue when I was loco foreman. They were starting to talk to us as if we shouldn't or didn't exist. You weren't in a position to do anything about it. They'd tell you to bugger off. They'd say, 'I'm not going on that one today.' You weren't allowed to send anyone home because they'd claim a day's pay and the boss would want to know what you were playing at. You'd tell them to go with a certain driver and they'd say, 'I'm not going with that old fool.' It got very awkward in the end. Once you gave in to one or two who would start arguing, the rest would jump on the bandwagon. I think the young were getting their attitude from films and television, watching and aping tough guys like James Cagney. Years ago you'd just send them home and tell them to come and see the boss in the morning.

Fred Bateman

Losing Steam

Working life changed quickly as the art of steam faded away. We had fifty engines in the shed at one time and only two steam raisers. Engines only stood at 80 lbs pressure. They'd just

Fred Bateman as Bletchley Traction Arranger in the late 1950s. He noted that the job was more difficult as young men modelled themselves more on film tough guys. (FB)

need a shovel and a barrow-load of coal under the door. When the fireman came, he pushed that forward over the boxes and the fires livened up. They were off the shed in about half an hour. Steam raisers had about three rows of engines each. They walked around checking the water. Engines would stand all night with water just bobbing. Just a matter of keeping the right pressure.

If you filled the fire boxes they'd hold a couple of tons. Sometimes we filled them right up and went for miles. You'd shut the door and forget it. Only trouble

A Duchess class loco, *Sir William Stanier* FRS, letting off steam near the flyover, 7 July 1964. (CS)

with heavy firing was it caused clinkering up. If you fired it just right and kept firing, you kept it clean. If you had just a film of smoke it was perfect combustion. Black smoke defeated the object of the superheated tubes because the gases from thick black smoke never heated the tubes like they should have done. If it was an incandescent fire the heat would liven the steam up and it would be a different engine. But drivers weren't much bothered which way you fired. Old 'Boxer' Milburn, though, he'd be waiting for you next morning if you'd been heavy firing: 'Don't you bring that engine in here like that again!' I had to knock it all out. The old engines they had to shovel out but the last ones they built, like the 9Fs, had proper grates – they could just shake it up and tip it out.

I've filled the old steam engines up, especially if I had good coal. We used to fill up under the elevator at Cambridge and that went all the way to Oxford. Eric Peacock who relieved me at Oxford said he never had to put any more in until he got back to Bicester coming back.

Diesels were a bit easier. I remember old Bob Berry with me on one of those Big Ds coming down a quarter of an hour late leaving Euston. He wasn't an ardent fan of speed. It was the old 10001. We were coming down Willesden and getting on the straight towards Wembley. It was first stop Watford on the down fast, 11.56 p.m. out of Euston. Bob came across with his light and said: 'What speed are you doing, you bloody fools? You'll get had for low flying soon!' We'd got about 97 mph on the clock. I said we'd better make time up and we'd got a bit left. The intention was to get into Bletchley at the right time for the passengers' sake. There was a sort of feeling about it – there's not much of that now.

Fred Bateman

Privatization

Before privatization, when I was an area controller, if an engine was in bad nick and a freight train came along we could put it in the loop and pinch the loco because we were all one company. It gave the passengers priority. The job was done in twenty-five minutes and the passengers were on their way. The freight train was the lesser requirement. We could find another loco for the freight later because we were all British Rail. Now, I was recently talking to one of my old colleagues. They had a loco fail at Stoke Hammond only a mile away. They'd got three locos behind the station buildings, big diesels suitable to take this train to Wolverhampton. It was taboo because it belonged to a different company. So the company that owned this express sent a locomotive from Crewe and the passengers were standing at Stoke Hammond for an hour and forty minutes waiting. The job could have been cleared up in twenty minutes. Nationalization had been good because you came to feel you were all one.

Fred Bateman

Nasty Business

My years as traffic manager were interesting and varied. I was called

Fred Bateman waits with his brick train at Calvert sidings, late 1950s. (FB)

out to incidents like the engine that went down the bank and blocked the line. I've seen no end of people cut up and was often the first on site. In the tunnel it's a nasty business. The first time I'd seen bodies was when platelayers were knocked over. I got used to it. First time I got a call, a fellow had committed suicide halfway down Tring cutting, down by Pitstone cement works. The police wouldn't come until I'd been. It was my job to clear the line and get trains running providing I didn't suspect anything – you know, foul play. Then, obviously it was for the police. The driver would report – for example at Leighton one woman just stood up on the track, her arms in the air, waiting. You knew there was nothing untoward. It would have been worse for me if it had been children or colleagues. Most were suicides.

Fred Bateman

Job for Life

I was made redundant in 1966. When you went on the railway you thought you had a job for life. The old boys said a young chap like that won't stay here five minutes but in the end I was earning bonuses for them. The track was in bad condition after the war and it was hard work for little. I got up to about £4 8s bonus.

We had our moments, taking the mickey out of each other. I started when I came out of the army just after the war. The majority of the branch was unfit for services, but they kept patching it up. Then in 1948-49 concrete sleepers came in and saved a lot of work. All the inspectors for the branch were based at Bletchley. The bosses were pleasant, they'd come up through the ranks. It took twenty-two men to lift a rail; it worked out to 75 lbs each. Old Ernie Dickens used to say when we were about to lift: 'Littl'uns in the middle.' I had a double hernia so you can tell it was heavy going. I worked hard and got top bonus so many times that they queried it at Northampton where they checked the sheets. When I went to hospital with the double hernia the surgeon said, 'Does your job involve very hard work?' I said, 'Yes, but the trouble is passengers don't see it because when the train goes by you're always standing still!'

My basic pay was just under £14 a week when I finished in 1966. If you used one of their shovels to lift ballast into a wagon you'd got a good weight. The surgeon did my first hernia and said it'd never come out. He was right, he did a good job. They said it would be three months before I was fit for work but I made it back in six and a half weeks. I was fit and wanted to get back. I went all over the district flagging for six months – getting all the allowances I was far better off. That was in 1961. The job was a religion. The good mates helped each other, sharing what they'd grown in their allotments or catching you a rabbit. A rabbit was worth six shillings at the butcher's and a hare seven and six. Yes, the job was more a religion than a way of life.

Des Tunks

CHAPTER 3
Just the job

Tommy Read (front right) makes a presentation to a retiring brick worker at Bletchley, *c.* 1922. (GL)

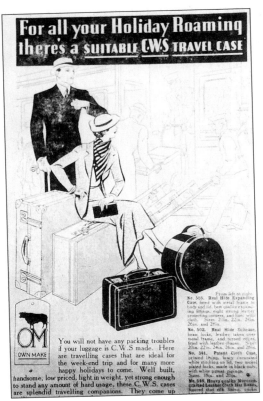

For all your Holiday Roaming there's a SUITABLE C.W.S TRAVEL CASE

OWN MAKE

You will not have any packing troubles if your luggage is C.W.S made. Here are travelling cases that are ideal for the week-end trip and for many more happy holidays to come. Well built, handsome, low priced, light in weight, yet strong enough to stand any amount of hard usage, these C.W.S. cases are splendid travelling companions. They come up

No. 505. Real Hide Expanding Case, fitted with serial frame in body and lid, best quality expanding lining, eight strong leather protecting corners, and lined with cloth. Sizes 20in, 22in, 24in, 26in, and 28in.
No. 502. Real Hide Suitcase, brass locks, leather taken over metal frame, and turned edges, fitted with leather chapes. Sizes 20in, 22in, 24in, 26in, and 28in.
No. 341. Patent Cloth Case, printed lining, fancy decorated white stitching on lid, two nickel plated locks, made in black only, with white patent pipings. Sizes 18in, and 20in.
No. 540. Heavy quality Morocco-grained Leather Cloth Hat Boxes, figured shot silk lining, pockets

The current style, as advertised by Bletchley Co-op, 1930s. (RONS)

Hope it's the Co-op

When I started working at the Co-op, aged fourteen, I had to pass an exam. A friend of mine who lived nearby worked with me. One morning we heard the fire engines. 'Oh, ain't it lovely,' we said. 'Hope it's the Co-op, then we won't have to do any work!' When we got there it was the Co-op and we had even more work to do. They set us on sorting out all the stuff, salvaging. We were on that for about a week, getting black from head to foot. It was dreadful – it was one of those things I wished I'd never said.

Gwen Akins

Sights

A lot of cattle were driven along country roads from farms to Bletchley market next to Duncombe Street. Some animals came by rail. The old drovers were quite characters, knowing just how to handle wayward animals which sometimes charged off down sidestreets and into people's gardens. Such events added to the excitement on our way to school.

Martin Blane

The gas lamps were a sight up to the early 1930s when electricity came in. John Breedon was the last lighter I remember. He had a long rod to unhook and open a door in the lamp, then he turned up a tap to bring the light on. There was a pilot light on all the time. He had to turn them all off again next morning.

Gwen Akins

The gas works where coal gas was produced was especially important to supply Fenny Stratford, Simpson and Bletchley because electricity did not come in until 1930. Gas was used in most homes for lighting and cooking. The engineer, manager and secretary of the Fenny Stratford Gas Light and Coke Company, Mr Jasper Cook, lived at Ivydene in the High Street, near the gas works entrance. The office was part of the house on the canal side.

Donald Fraser Blane

The Co-op, seventies-style. (RC)

Housework

I had set jobs like polishing the hall and chairs and darning socks. I hated that. I had to do housework for mum's friend. My father, Frank Burridge, was a kind, gentle man. He worked hard on his garden and had to sell his spare vegetables to neighbours and shopkeepers.

Gwen Akins

Blacksmith

William Webster and his partner Harry Keyte ran a blacksmith's business at the top of Duncombe Street. It backed onto the main railway line opposite where Sainsbury's is now. The building is still there, although it has been a garage for many years. The two partners ran the smithy at the turn of the century until about 1908 when William, his wife Sarah and nine of their twelve children emigrated like so many others at the time to Canada, finally settling in the Victoria area of Vancouver Island in 1910 where they set up another successful blacksmith's business.

Daphne R. Atkins

Half a Pound of Cadbury's

I did all my training at the Co-op. When the sales were on I learned the drapery side of it. They built another confectionery shop where I ended up as manageress. I had to do all the buying. They had to send in their orders to me from Winslow, Steeple Claydon and all the village shops. The bakers came in as

William Webster and Harry Keyte's blacksmith's shop at the top of Duncombe Street. They ran the smithy until William and his wife, Sarah, emigrated to Canada in 1908, where they settled in the Victoria area of Vancouver Island. (DRA)

well. We were packing for about thirteen shops and the vans. I had some funny experiences. This lady happened to be on the Co-op committee. She put me in quite a predicament. It wasn't open plan then. Across your sweets was a glass top and I was serving and happened to glance round and see this lady take a half-pound block of chocolate and put it in her basket. I thought, what should I do? She's old and on the committee. If I'm nasty she'll report me and they won't believe me against her. We had no computers, only old-fashioned tills. When she came up she took her things out, put them on the counter and I started putting them down. I got nearly to the end and I thought I should say something. I said I should just take for the half-pound of Cadbury's milk she had in her basket. She took it and gave it to me, never blushed or said a word, and no more was heard.

Gwen Akins

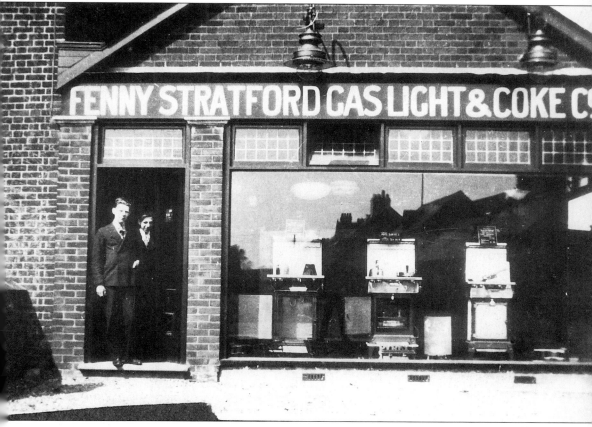

The offices of the Fenny Stratford Gas Light and Coke Company, formerly Still's Grammar School, on the corner of Cambridge Street and Queensway in 1928. Donald Blane and Jack Robinson are in the doorway. (DFB)

Office Boy

Mr Jasper Cook gave me the job of office boy at the gas works in 1923. The gas company would install a supply of gas with a prepayment slot, three lights and a cooking stove free of cost. The coin meters (usually for pennies), which were used by two-thirds of householders, were set to deliver slightly less than the coin value so that when the money was collected and the metered volume read, there was a surplus to be handed back to the householder. The company collector took about one month to make the full round, calling every three months. He was accompanied by a youth who was left in charge of the 'copper truck' (a strong box on a chassis with tyred wheels) which he pushed. The collector was always welcomed in because the housewife would anticipate the rebate money – in many cases it would represent a new pair of shoes or a hat. The coin box would be unlocked from the meter and tipped out onto the kitchen table, provoking many covetous comments! The collector would count the pennies into stacks of twelve and

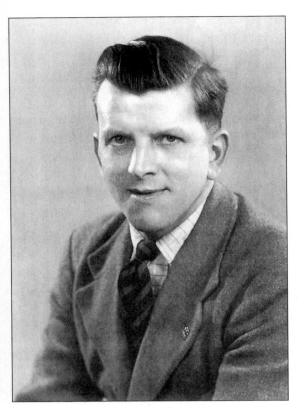

Ron Staniford, c. 1933. (RONS)

then put them into blue paper bags of sixty (five shillings' worth). I believe that each bag would have weighed a pound and a half. The average home would have £2 in pennies, so the weight would be 12 lbs. The collector had to transfer the money to the Copper Truck. Although everyone knew there was cash in the Copper Truck there was no instance of robbery.

Donald Fraser Blane

Babies' Bonnets

Miss Laura Haring, the girls' school headmistress, was a great character. She used to breed Angora

rabbits and when she clipped them we had to spin it and someone else knitted it – by which time it was pretty grubby! There were fifty-eight pupils in my class at Standard VII.

Jean Raiders (née Smith)

A Local Newspaper

My aunt and grandmother kept a biggish shop at 61 Aylesbury Street. There was some talk of me taking it over, but my parents thought it was too big a responsibility for a boy of sixteen. So I went to a stationery firm, a wholesalers in Northampton. I stuck it for about three years and got very fed up. In the meantime I got to know very well the printer Harold Price who had a little printing business in Bletchley Road (now Queensway). We talked about the need for a local newspaper.

All we had was the *North Bucks Times* which was published in Leighton Buzzard, Bedfordshire. It was really a reprint of the *Leighton Observer* with one page altered and a little bit of Bletchley news stuck in. So Harold and I decided, without any money at all, to start a local newspaper. We needed an existing firm to print it, which meant trailing round. In the end the Bedfordshire Times Publishing Company agreed to print it. We called our new paper *The Bletchley Gazette*. I did all the editorial except for my partner Harold, who had to give much of his time to his printing business. He wrote leading articles and the children's column. I did the rest, collected all the news. I didn't know any shorthand. I made brief notes and relied on memory which a think was better than getting tied down in too much detail. In my experience that made for a broad picture and made a better story.

I can still remember the excitement on that first Friday night when the first edition was being published. I had a little broken-down Austin Seven, drove up to the station and picked up these parcels of papers, distributed them to local newsagents and then waited to see if they sold. They did. We sold 1,500. Bearing in mind Bletchley's population was about 5,000, that was good. We catered for Bletchley and the surrounding villages, going on to make steady progress.

It was soon clear that we couldn't afford the prices the *Bedfordshire Times* charged for printing. So we decided to do it ourselves. This involved buying an intertype printing machine and a flat bed printing machine. In those days a linotype machine was well over £1,000 which we hadn't got. A printing machine was £7,000-£8,000. We explored around and then went up to the Intertype HQ in our little green Austin for an appointment with the managing director. We were escorted into a palatial office and told him we wanted an intertype machine but we'd got no money. What could he do about it? By the time we came out, he'd sold us an intertype machine brand new, for payments over four years. That was the first stage. We then had to get a flat bed printing machine. We went to a firm in London that had got a machine that had been thrown out by De La Rue, the postage stamp printers. The machine was dead accurate. He sold it to us for £250 payable over two years. So in June 1934 we had our very first *Bletchley*

Gazette printed and published in Bletchley.

We had to employ a full-time operator. Setting was a full-time job. I took an assistant, Greville Trumpfield, who went on to become registrar of births, marriages and deaths in North Bucks. He came as a boy. We took on a derelict shed next to where Harold Price lived. We had been occupying a little hut which we called the office, at the bottom of Harold's garden. The shed was next door and a part of a building which became the Central Garage. We rented it and started up.

We made one bad mistake. The gas company had been a major advertiser and we fell for the manager's suggestion to install a gas engine to run our printing machine. We had some sweaty times over that engine, but we printed every week, sometimes running through the night. We couldn't afford any more machines and so did hand folding. Strictly illegal, my assistant working through the night, but we did, then we loaded the papers into my car and delivered them to the newsagent. We never thought of giving up. We struggled through. The printing business was building up too. How many hours I workied I don't know. I never counted. My parents thought I was mad.

Ron Staniford

Bletchley Brickworks

I started at Bletchley brickworks in 1935 when Tommy Reid still owned it. I was an apprentice bricklayer in Woburn. Jack West taught me and when he went to LBC in Bletchley he

RB135 'Navvy' being assembled at Bletchley Knothole, June or July 1930. The old hand-cut benches and makeshift railway are visible in the background. (JB)

said there'd be a job for me if I wanted. Sulphur fumes from the chimneys never bothered me. I can't remember anyone ever getting into trouble over it. They reckoned the first place they ever got the fumes was across the North Sea.

Bubbles Field

Cycling In From Linslade

The original brickmaking was done across the road from where the works finished up. The original pit filled with water and became a fishing site. Bricks were hand made then and cut with wire, starting about 100 years ago.

I started in the ticket office in 1935, cycling in from Linslade to begin with, getting to the office around six in the morning. Some fellows cycled further, rain or shine. Until 1937, deliveries were made by outside hauliers. They'd be queuing up to get in on a Saturday morning.

Reg Knapp

Lucky the Timekeeper was Out

One of the biggest accidents was when I arrived one morning. There were railway trucks over on their side in their yard. They'd been shunted in too fast, pushed the stop buffers over, run across the yard, demolished the timekeeper's office and knocked a corner of the despatch office. One or two ended up in Newton Road. Lucky the timekeeper was out! I handed out delivery tickets with my overcoat on that morning!

When I first started, there was a stable and a horse and cart was being used. The driver was Fred Cook. All bricks were put into kilns by barrows handled by two setters, forty bricks to a barrow. The drawers used to pull them out after two weeks' burning.

Reg Knapp

They Were Brick Workers

In the old days the blokes were real brick workers. You'd find the same on the railway, but there aren't many what you'd call railwaymen today. Our clay pit worked on a bench system, using a racking arm or drag line. There was a bend half way down because our pit was so deep. The valuable clay was at the bottom where the drag line couldn't reach, so the racking arm worked up the pit and the drag line down it.

Jack Bromfield

Sweat

Sweat used to run off the men drawing the bricks out of the kilns – they worked in 100 degrees Fahrenheit. While some kilns were being emptied others were filled with fresh bricks. Filling the kilns was called setting and they did it by hand before the war. Waste heat from kiln fires was channelled ahead through ducts to dry the fresh ones ready for burning. It was a continuous process. When the fire reached them they caught light easily and burned themselves because the clay was full of carbon. They only needed a bit of smudge-coal dust to control the temperature. These bricks were called Flettons because that was the first place where this deep clay was used. It was so hard and dry that they had to grind it down into a dust before pressing the bricks into shape with these very strong presses. They were pressed four times which is why the London Brick Company, which took over Bletchley brickworks, called them 'Phorpres' bricks.

Better Off than King or Queen

One old brickyard worker, 'Jimmy Dig Deeper', would choose one of the warm empty kilns to sleep in. He went missing once. They thought he'd been bricked in and burned with a load of new bricks. His job was to tar the walls inside the kilns. A big old colonial boy, no-one knew his age. Nearly sixteen stone he was. Lovely old fellow. He used barrels and barrels of tar and a big, old, long brush. By the time he got round one set of kilns it was time to start another. Living in the kilns, he said, made him better off than king or queen because he had a different room every night. He slept in one of the old cockney barrows they used for getting the bricks out on.

Bubbles Field

Skinning Cheeses and Cleaning Coppers

I left school at fourteen to work at the Co-op delivering milk in the mornings. We had a large milk churn and a bucket with a half-pint measure. In the afternoon I worked in the grocery skinning cheeses and cleaning coppers after we'd boiled the ham. I remember a very bad winter in 1933. That March I joined the London Brick Company on 15s a week as an office boy. Ted Lacey was the timekeeper.

The men's lavatory was on the edge of the knot hole (clay pit). This was a line of cubicles with boards over the buckets. The doors were removed because Jack Bedford said night workers slept in them. We had no proper canteen, just a long hut with tables and chairs.

Jack Blane

A Lasting Impression

I worked at Bletchley Flettons which wasn't as sophisticated as London Brick. I asked the foreman where the lavatories were and the foreman pointed across a field. When I got there I found a long piece of wood – it had still got the bark on. It was one way of discouraging you from wasting time in the loo. I must say those lavatories made a lasting impression on me and probably on my bottom as well!

Ray Akins

Deprived Childhood?

You could get everything from the Co-op. They had a milk and coal round and sold everything from clothes to dining room suites. I started evening work at Pacey's ironmonger's in Fenny Stratford, as a delivery boy, riding a bike with a basket for the paraffin. They paid 12s 6d a week around 1945. I saved for a new bike. I didn't have a deprived childhood. If we wanted something we did swaps.

Our headmaster was Mr Cook, nicknamed Barrel because he was rotund. Being an Oxford man he rolled his 'r's. He whacked pupils but that was understandable. If you were late after the whistle blew you were marched into Billy Bennet's shop. There were no excuses, just whack, whack, whack! You accepted that.

Rolly Doggett

A Green Man

Fred Barret was foreman when Jim Reid got me a job with him at Bletchley Flettons. I cycled over from Norfolk on the Friday. The Saturday morning Jim had spoken to the foreman and they set me on straight away. I was put with the callow gang, the job being to remove the overburden of clay. It was a wonderful job, they were all original Bucks agricultural workers. They had a local cricket team. I couldn't play but they tried me out. I was there for about eleven months and found out that my Fenlander lingo amused them. They used to rib me about it. After I'd been there about three months most of what they said was in the same lingo so it must have been a rather strong influence.

We had one robust chap on the gang as big as me and in those days we both fancied ourselves. His name was Horace. They all got called off one day to help get one of the locos back on the rails, leaving me in charge of the tip and to make a cup of tea for their return. Horace, a great old beefy chap, said, 'I'd like mine weak.' By some unforeseen happening it turned out to be extra strong because they were a bit late back. So I had an experience which I had only previously had in the Bay of Bengal, seeing a man go green. He looked so ill that I thought we were going to lose him.

They were wonderful days and I was sorry they were brought to a close, but I thought six long days or five long nights a week was enough and didn't work Sundays. I've got to say the foreman was very good about it because I wouldn't work on a Sunday and told him why. He said, 'There's only one thing, Akins: if they all worked as hard as you we shouldn't need any Sunday work.' That mollified me a bit and I didn't have trouble getting another job.

I did refuse selling ice cream which was more Sunday work. I remember this chit of a girl behind the Labour Exchange counter: 'I'll stop your dole, I'll stop your dole,' she said. So I said, 'I'll get another job.' So I took a temporary job with the railway rounding up horses, which terrified me! Then loading them into wagons and watering them. Unloading the odd load of bullocks was also nerve-wracking because they were always wild when they'd had a railway journey.

Brickyard workers Arthur Bowler, Sid Wenman, Frank Barnes and Ken Mote rest from their job of drawing bricks from Kiln 8 by hand, before the Second World War. (KM)

I also missed the novelty of the brickworks' toilets in that old iron building across the fields. Not that I ever wasted much time crossing that field to get there. There weren't even any cubicles. You sat in a line. It was a pretty dire experience and you had to be desperate.

Ray Akins

Pound of Flesh

Mr Hersee, the London Brick Company works manager, was a

Ted Hersee (left), the brickyard manager, presents a retirement gift to ticket clerk Stan Parrot in the 1950s. (RK)

One of the Fortunate Ones

I was an apprentice shoe repairer which lasted till I was twenty-one. I was fourteen when I started. When you look at the speed of learning today you realize that apprenticeships were cheap labour. In the thirties you took what was there. There was no choice or benefits. You took what was available. Your parents couldn't support you. Lots of boys started off doing errands for a few bob. I did two jobs when I started and got 5s a week. I did a paper round. I had to pay mum back a bit a week for my bicycle she'd bought. It made long hours. Life was getting a bit boring when the war came. I was one of the fortunate ones, going into the RAF. I volunteered before I was due for call-up which meant I had a bit of choice what I went into. I chose the RAF. I was sad to leave my pals and cycling. I did my technical training at Halton. We did our foot drill at RAF Melsham but I missed most of that because they asked if anyone could play a bugle. I'd played in the Boy Scouts. They said this was good, so a little group of us played in the bugle band on the march. I didn't do much squarebashing. We used to wander off to the back of the parade ground and do our little bit of practice.

At that stage they were in such a hurry to get people trained we only did four weeks' basic. I went to Northampton for my medical and to Penarth in Wales for an aptitude test. They set you a few little sums, interviewed you and I passed. They said they'd put me down for airframes as a rigger. That's when I went to Malton. They were so pushed, if you passed out with a certain mark they put you on a

grand chappie but he wanted his pound of flesh. Apart from that he treated the chappies all right. If he caught a chappie doing something wrong he wouldn't say, 'You're going to have the sack.' The London Brick Company got me out of the army as soon as the war finished, to help rebuild the kilns which had disintegrated because the works had been shut down and used for munitions. There were still German prisoners and later on European Volunteer Workers helping to get things going again. I got on all right with the Germans. They had a hostel at Drayton Parslow.

Bubbles Field

The London Brick Company's Morris Commercial lorry P89 loaded up at Bletchley works, early 1950s. (JB)

fitter's course. I qualified A1 and carried on to another course going up to Kinloss in Scotland for eight months. I was posted to India, our ship being torpedoed and sunk on the way. But eventually we got there. I was a corporal on the plains of India. We had two weeks' leave in the foothills of the Himalayas, 8,000 feet up. We were out there two and a half years.

Martin Blane

Delivering the Bricks

After the war I wanted to carry on flying but before I could get a civilian qualification to work in the post office air service they were taken over by the nationalized British European Airways. Eventually I ended up driving lorries delivering bricks for the London Brick Company. You started out driving the Morris Commercials, with about 2,000 bricks on the back. They had

AEC Mammoth Major eight-wheeler with driver 'Wacker' Stokes ready for an early start after a night at the White Café on the old Brighton Road, mid-1950s. (JB)

petrol engines and were pretty nippy empty. After two years I put in for relief eight-wheeler driving. A lot of blokes didn't want this because they'd have to spend at least two nights away from home, starting at six in the morning. You were limited to 20 mph. There were a lot of south coast runs, including Kent and Essex. There was a lot of rebuilding and expansion of towns going on. The speed limit increased in the sixties and they started using forklifts on loading. When we were allowed up to 40 mph we got a lot further in our eleven hours' driving time.

Jack Bromfield

A Terror

When I started they wouldn't employ you unless you'd do sixty-six hours a week, including Saturdays. Dennis Samuel, the traffic foreman, was a terror. He had been on holiday near Chichester when Chrissy Johnson called me in and said, 'You've booked this run about six miles too far.' Chrissy was transport manager. Dennis was there, so I said, 'Been on your holidays again, Sam?' So Dennis went a little bit red. He used to hop about from one leg to the other and scratch his behind. 'Well, chap,' he used to say as he explained the 'better' route. So I said, 'Oh, so you want me to go that way in future?' So I talked them into sending Sam with me. We got near Selsey Bill where I knew the fun would start. There were big red iron triangles on a post. I said, 'I can't go over that bridge – there's a six-ton limit.' He said, 'But you can pop over this time.' I said, 'No chance,' and had to reverse about half a mile. It was so late by the time we unloaded, my eleven hours were up. I said, 'She's all yours, Sam.' He said, 'I'm not going to drive that.' But I just thought, 'You've been having a go at me, now you either drive it or you don't – eighty miles all through London.' I suspected this might happen and had brought my night kit. Sam had a miserable night!

Jack Bromfield

CHAPTER 4
Pure enjoyment

Kathleen Tarbox (left), the coal merchant's wife, and Mrs Eileen Chappell (far right), mid-1930s. (ST)

Pipe Majors at Manor Fields, just off the A5, in June 1966. (RK)

Jam Jars

Outside the school some days there'd be a man who wanted jam jars. He made paper windmills for people. We all thought they were lovely so we'd go home to mum and beg as many jam jars as possible so we could get one of these paper windmills.

Gwen Akins

Dagenham Girl Pipers

I founded Bletchley brickworks sports club in 1931, with Ted Hersee, because there was nothing to do. Thousands came to works sports days.

The company provided buses because there weren't the cars or television. The Dagenham Girl Pipers came to one sports day. Bletchley had one of the finest football teams in the Midlands and we won the national tug-o'-war championships at White City.

Jim White

Waxworks

The market was held in the street and also Fenny fair which reached from Wells' shop to where Makeham lived. I can remember a big waxworks show standing outside Brett's shop. Where the old pump stood there was a

The manager of Bletchley brickworks, Roger Lyle, presents the cup to winning bowls captain Jim White after the match against London Transport in 1960. (JW)

big swingboat; about a dozen got in at a time, I think we paid a halfpenny each.

Emily Fennemore, writing in 1949

Emily Fennemore was the first of eight children of Frank and Sarah Howard who were married at Simpson church in September 1872. In 1893 she married Edmund Fennemore who started the undertaking business of E. Fennemore & Son. Their son Ernest died in the battle for Passchendaele in August 1917, but the business is carried on by their grandson, Ernest Allen. In Aunt Em's childhood, in the 1870s, Fenny Stratford would have been much as it had been for centuries.

Jean Raiders (née Smith)

A Pillar of Society

My father, Frank Burridge, was a steward in the church and a pillar of society, but at the annual sports day cycle races he'd be shouting: 'Go on, Bill, knock him off, cut across, go on, go on!' He used to get so excited. That was in the 'rec' by Watling Street, near the old swimming pool. Being a Methodist he wasn't supposed to gamble. I think when mum wasn't looking he bought a ticket. It only cost him a tanner and he won a new bicycle.

Gwen Akins

Frank wished he hadn't won that bike. His life wasn't worth living, he didn't half cop it. I'd have sold it on my way home myself.

Ray Akins

Prizes

My brother, Bob, won three first prizes one year at the annual cycle races. They were all worth ten guineas. That was a lot of money in those days. One big item was a grandfather clock.

Martin Blane

Lord and 'Fanny' Lady Leon

Lord and 'Fanny' Lady Leon owned Bletchley Park before the war. During the season we used to follow the hunt, opening the gates for them, hoping for a tip. The estate then stretched from the Bletchley to Buckingham road right across to Denbigh Road. They hunted right across it. On August Bank Holiday Monday they held one of the biggest shows in the county, with athletics, cycle racing, a gymkhana, flower shows, arts and crafts, sheep dog trials – just about everything.

Martin Blane

Seaside

My parents took me and my four brothers to the seaside every year, mainly because dad worked on the railway and they got three free passes a year. We usually went to London each year – then, a chocolate éclair was a special treat. I usually had a birthday party with jelly and blancmange. There were two picture houses. I've shed my memory of all the films except Sanders of the River with Paul Robeson. I saw

that four times.

Gwen Akins

Christmas in the Oven

We had a dog when I was a kid. Our dog used to fight every other dog that came into the road. Nearly every kid kept chickens. One time I had some rabbits. Often they'd end up in the pot. At Christmas everybody had a cockerel. Through the year you'd hear a chorus of cockerels in the road. Then come Christmas it was dead quiet. Cockerels were busy celebrating Christmas in the oven.

Martin Blane

Going Fishing

In the thirties we used to cycle from Winslow to Bletchley for the ride. We used to get fish and chips and come home again. We raced a thunderstorm one night because someone told us lightning could strike your handlebars.

Gladys Close

Songs on Sunday

One of the signalmen at Bletchley, Arthur Quimby, when they got those microphones fitted in No. 5 yard for shunting, every Sunday night he used to whistle hymns – you could hear it all over Bletchley. That was just after the war. It was a ritual when I was foreman in the old steam shed. I used to

Bletchley children enjoy the peace celebrations, 1945. (RL)

get up and listen to Arthur whistling hymns.

Fred Bateman

Alice in Wonderland

Our new house at 30 Leon Road was very nice. My mum inherited some money. It cost about £600. I liked books, especially *Alice in Wonderland* and *Little Women*. I liked playing billiards and picnics were very nice in summer. We played hopscotch, skipping, chase and hide and seek in the street or rec. We rarely played in the garden – we went for walks in the woods. My special friends were Rosa, Vera, Dorothy and several boys.

Gwen Akins

Striped Blazers

Donald Lord was the police superintendent's son. He ran an entertainments agency and played with his band towards the end of the war. They wore striped blazers. He bought a bulk lot of Barrathea material to make them. His double bass was bigger than him. Not many knew the right dance step for quick step or foxtrot. I took lessons.

Martin Blane

Champion Ploughman

My father worked at Leys Farm, just over the canal bridge at Water Eaton, owned by William Gurney. I believe the water mill formed part of the

Bletchley Rhythm keep the town dancing at Wilton in the 1950s. (RL)

farm. I remember that during the 1940s my father won a cup as champion ploughman in a competition nearby.

Daphne R. Atkins

Things We Used to Do

We used to go down the Newfoundout and take engine numbers. I fell in once and got a right telling off from my mother. We used to see the mail train go by and drop the mail into a net. Christmas time you usually had a stocking, usually one of your dad's. That was filled with nuts, oranges, sweets, perhaps a story book and a bit of plasticene in later years. I remember a little train set from Woolworths. Everything there was threepence or sixpence. They had all the bits. But the nearest Woolworths when I was a boy was Aylesbury or Northampton. There were only three shops in Bletchley Road; it was just as

easy to go by train to Northampton. Nash's was the only local toyshop.

We had our seasons for games. Conkers didn't cost much, and there were hoops and marbles. Nothing very elaborate, you made your own fun. When everybody's in the same boat no-one takes any notice. But nowadays if somebody's got something a bit better it makes envy.

Martin Blane

Ringing the Bell

I was once badly frightened, deservedly so, by a policeman. St Martin's mission church was situated where Brooklands Road joins Queensway. There was a bell under a shelter on the roof. Local boys used to throw stones to try to hit the bell. One day I threw a stone – it did not hit the bell but broke a church window. A nearby policeman heard the glass break and came down to

Early twentieth-century shops in Bletchley Road (now Queensway). (MB)

Brooklands Road where I was trying to hide. He took me home and said I might have to go to the police court and pay damages. After a few days I was told to go to the vicarage and see the Revd J. Firminger. After I said I was sorry and would not do it again he counselled me and I was free to go.

Donald Fraser Blane

Winter Warmers

One thing we did in winter was make a winter warmer. We got a treacle tin, punched holes in the sides, fixed a handle on and then lit a bit of wood, coke or coal inside. We swung it round and round on a wire. Then we had a little fire to warm our hands on.

We spent a lot of time outside.

Martin Blane

Gas-Lit Stalls

In a field near where the Leisure Centre was built they held a market with gas-lit stalls in the winter. They used 'tilly lamps' as we called them. This same field next to the New Inn was where they held big funfairs and circuses. It was the highlight of the town. We liked Angel Dindol's shop too. It had an angel statue in a niche out front. Dindol was a Jew who sold clothes before the war.

Martin Blane

Good Shops

We had some good shops. Yeo's had an old style drapery. His window displays always included models draped in clothes old-fashioned even then. He always took care there was no erotic exposure. It was just the place to buy your directoire knickers (passion killers)!

Martin Blane

During the war, while I was still at school, a landmine was dropped somewhere between Woburn and Fenny Stratford. The blast broke one of Yeo's windows and knocked one of his models over, which had its funny side, I suppose! I think they were actually after the aerodrome at Cranfield though.

Ken Southwell

The Boss

Before the war Sir Malcolm Stewart was the boss at the London Brick Company. He phoned Bletchley works manager Ted Hersee to say he didn't realize there was a works tug-o'-war team. He asked how these fellows trained. Hersee said, 'All in their own time,' afraid to let Sir Malcolm know he gave us a few hours. 'Well, from now on these men will train in the works' time,' he said. We were a good advert for the firm. We had a lovely sports ground. Hersee had it built special with a pavilion for a drink at night.

Bubbles Field

Homely and Happy

There was an annual family day at the brickworks sports ground. It was always very successful and of course there were Christmas parties with presents given by Father Christmas. It was all very homely and happy. Lots of commendation would be given to Jim White, head of despatch, for all the hard work he did on the social side at the works.

Reg Knapp

Happy Motoring

My first car was a Morris 8. It cost me £200. It was the only one that had a personality. It invariably broke down when we planned to visit my mother-in-law at Bletchley.

Ray Akins

You didn't see many cars. I remember when we went to Woburn Sands by horse and cart. The teachers took buns and a big tin of sweets. They threw them up in the air and we had to scramble for them. Then they put up long trestle tables and put out all these cakes. There was a lady used to come every year with her boys. I noticed that every year she'd got her loose coat on. She was a gypsy-like lady and shifted cakes into her raincoat pocket like mad.

Gwen Akins

A good, old fashioned day out at Bletchley brickworks sports day in the early 1950s. The author as a baby is with his parents on the back row. (JW)

Courting and Sparking

We were introduced by Gwen's father whose duty it was to stand by the church door and introduce people. We first met when Gwen was in the choir.

Ray Akins

The fashion was to wear black at church. My little brother was sitting with me in the choir and Ray looked at me. He thought, 'Oh, what a shame, she's a widow so young!' I looked at Ray; I didn't know him. He was sitting with the Co-op coal man, his wife and his daughter, Marjorie Hall. I didn't take much notice. I thought he looked all right, sort of thing, thinking he was Marjorie Hall's boyfriend, until one

night when we were coming out of chapel, father introduced me.

Gwen Akins

When her dad introduced us, I said I'd got a meal to get, and Gwen said, 'Which way are you going?' I said, 'Down Bletchley Road,' and she said, 'So am I,' and I walked her home. All we talked about was that we'd both decided not to get married. What made us discuss that I don't know, but here's the result and I've never regretted it. I moved to Bletchley after working at the brickworks around Peterborough. I'd got problems with my lodgings and thought I'd get out of the way. I went to Flettons Ltd at Bletchley. It wasn't long afterwards that I met Gwen Burridge and I've got in my diary for that day,

The London Brick Company's Christmas party for Bletchley employees' children, early 1950s. (JW)

'The last time' or 'The last one' or something like that because I'd already been rejected once.

Ray Akins

I never used to swear, but the first time was when I went out with Ray.

Gwen Akins

Gwen got her foot stuck where the cows had been and I had to pull her out. It went slurp and was all covered with blue. I won't tell you what she said, but there was a lot of force behind it!

Ray Akins

We had a side door at the house. Ray and I'd been having a little cuddle and kiss goodnight at ten o'clock and they used to open a window at the top and throw things down on us. In those days, you had to be in by ten o'clock. When I was young I liked so many boys and met plenty, having four brothers. Snowballing in the winter with them was fun. My first date was Ken Fuller. I went with him for several years. When he moved to London I visited him for a holiday. I was quite adventurous at seventeen.

Ray and I were married at Bletchley Road Methodist Chapel on 23 December 1939. The best man was Jock Stewart. My wedding dress was white brocade. Afterwards I had it dyed and spoilt it. My bridesmaids June and Irene wore long pink dresses with matching Dutch caps. I felt very nervous and worse still when I realized I'd left my going-away shoes at home. Our

Grandma Chappell enjoys a picnic near the canal, off Simpson Road, with 'Young Billy' Southwell (right) and Scamp, early 1930s. (ST)

reception was held in a hall nearby. We had a lovely meal and speeches. We couldn't go far away for honeymoon due to the war and my husband was likely to be called up. I got two days off and we went to Wiles Farm near Peterborough. Taxis and trains ran late due to fog. We stayed in lodgings for a few days until Rose Cottage was ready. On the first Sunday there I set light to the dinner and did I cry! Food was rationed and cooking was simple at that time. Most people observed the Sabbath then and shops and places of entertainment were closed.

Gwen Akins

Banging the Drum

The Boys' Brigade was run by Ron Staniford. On one occasion they were on a march from Fenny Stratford to Simpson, led by their band. Bill Burridge, my brother-in-law to be, was on the drum but decided to vary the timing. So he was demoted to walk at the back of the procession. This prompted him to cut a pole out of the hedge and march with his little pill-box hat perched on the top of it. He was too agile for Ron who must have been quite put out by mutiny in the ranks! But of course they finished up great friends. Bill showed no sign then that he would eventually become a Methodist minister.

Ray Akins

The Loveliest Time

Our daughter Gwyneth was born in April 1942 and Janice in August

Members of the local cycle group in the early 1930s. Martin Blane is front right. (MB)

1946, both at private nursing homes in Bletchley. They were so different. Gwyneth was studious and willing to help. Janice would sit and wait for Gwyneth to go upstairs and say, 'Bring me my pyjamas down please, Gwyneth.' They did fall out at times! Janice would get her words mixed up and called beetroot 'roobeet'. She pulled most of Ray's carrots up and set seeds of her own. The loveliest time with our daughter Gwyneth was when Ray came home from Burma and I took him to see Gwyneth asleep in her bed. He put his arms around me and said, 'Does she really belong to us?' She was nearly four.

Gwen Akins

Playing Shops

Playing shops was the children's favourite game. They spent hours selling me building bricks which were pretend doughnuts or cakes. Bringing up children, I learned the hard way not to worry too much if they don't want to eat. The doctor said they will eat when they are hungry. My husband loves drawing and drew them dot-to-dot pictures. He also decorated their bedroom with stars on the ceiling and walls with fairy scapes. Gwyneth always wanted to teach and became a head teacher. Janice was artistic and keen to get married young.

Gwen Akins

Happy Childhood

We lived in Napier Street. I had a happy childhood. I was an only child and I went to Bletchley Road school. There was a teacher there who'd taught in my father's day, Horace Buck.

Bletchley rugby players, late 1940s. (RL)

School life was pretty good. The school backed onto the 'Rec'. But I had such a good home life that I didn't want to be at school, and home was just across the road. Everything closed on Sunday so Sunday School was the only place to go. Good Friday and Easter were another world. I don't think even the cinemas opened.

Jenny Stacey

Real Battleaxe

We always had about thirty in class. You didn't dare speak in Miss Burn's class – she was a real battleaxe. She looked about ninety when she was teaching us. Her and her sister both taught, both spinsters. You could be really frightened of teachers then. I was always in the sports. Being tall, I could

run well.

There were no mixed-sex sports in the fifties. I liked netball. I was always in the sports, and being tall meant I could get into pubs easier. We had drinks at The Bell and The George.

Jenny Stacey

A Sea of Blossom

From the canal bridge at Simpson you could look down and view one sea of blossom – apples, pears and plums. It all had to be destroyed. We knew Milton Keynes was coming and couldn't stop it. We fought to make the best of it.

Baden Powell

Elmers Grammar School, *c.* 1930. (MH)

Pretty Shells

After the war we went away on holiday every year. Once we took the children to a band concert. There Janice crept onto the stage and was conducting. So the conductor gave her the baton to lead them. We liked to hunt for pretty beach shells to make into jewellery boxes.

Gwen Akins

Working Men's Club

After the pop concerts at Wilton Hall we'd go and collect our autograph books. We used to hand them in at the end of the stage before the show. You'd have your name in it so they could sign it to you.

The Working Men's Club had a dance on Wednesday evening. They had an upstairs room dedicated to music and kids' dancing. They just had records all the time. It was mainly railwaymen's children, twelve- or thirteen-year-olds. Ray Charles' *Lucky Old Sun* sticks in my mind. They used to have competitions during evenings as well but you had to get home before it got dark. There was no drinking and the boys would sit around the edge of the room watching the girls with their old petticoats puffing out those great big floral dresses and skirts, ponytails flying. That was the late 1950s and early 1960s. We thought we were the bee's knees. The boys wore drainpipes. The boys were boys, that's it – they were gawky.

Jenny Stacey

The Makarios

Evenings were spent at a café called Makarios near where they've built the multi-storey car park. It was run by

85

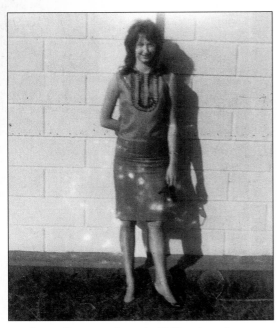

Jenny Stacey in the early 1960s, when the Rolling Stones brought an air of danger to the local teen scene. (JS)

a Greek man. It was just a coffee bar with a juke box. A cup of coffee would last you all night. We'd sit around talking and listening to the music – Del Shannon, Ricki Nelson I liked.

Jenny Stacey

Greenways

We weren't allowed in Greenways café, it was a rough one. The rockers went in there – their motorbikes were the best bit about them. I liked their style, the way they dressed. They were threatening, I suppose. They were fellas, that was it. I preferred motorbikes to scooters.

Jenny Stacey

Claudia Colbert in Studs

I remember somebody coming into the café and it was the old studded jeans thing. He'd got 'Claudia Colbert' written in studs up the side of his jeans. We hadn't a clue who she was. The café and cinema were our entertainment. That was it. The ballroom at Dunstable was the in thing. They had dances with all the top names. I think I only went there once because you couldn't get there very easily from Bletchley.

Jenny Stacey

Main Bands

Some big names came to Wilton Hall. My favourites were Elvis, Eddie Cochran and Rick Nelson, and sadly they never did come. Cliff Richard was a bit tame. But we had some big names, like The Hollies and Johnny Kidd and The Pirates. There was always a main band and a small band. We had the Stones of course. I was crushed right at the front. You couldn't move, and my friend felt faint and we had to go to the back. They were excellent. It was a noise, the in sound. The Beatles weren't to the fore then. The Stones were a bit wicked. It all sounded so much more naughty then, and seductive with the lights flashing. There was a sort of allure. Drugs were in the distance then except for the odd few.

Jenny Stacey

CHAPTER 5

Changing track

Has Railtrack run out of rails? This diesel railcar, L123, is leaving town by road in 1997 after service on the Bedford line, wearing original green livery and leased by North London Railways from Angel Trains. (RC)

Clun Castle, No. 7029, approaching Bletchley station on 27 March 1965. The driver is Fred Bateman. (DB)

One Extreme to the Other

W hen I was a boy growing up in the thirties it was a case of spare the rod and spoil the child. Unfortunately it has gone from one extreme to the other.

Martin Blane

Y ou could walk down the street in Bletchley and know everybody around you before the war.

Fred Bateman

O n Valentine's Day children used to come round and sing and on the first day of May they brought round their garlands and sang. All these customs have died out.

Emily Fennemore, writing in 1949

The Whistles would Blow

N ew Year's Eve everyone would listen to the engines whistle. There was always a lot of engines in the shed, and fitters with their mates. At midnight there was a set signal and the whistles would blow the New Year in. That all went out when steam went. They did it for a bit longer when I was traction arranger at the depot. You had about a dozen diesels and we all sat on diesels at midnight: 'Wah, wah, wah!' It didn't sound the same, not like the steam engines whistling 'On Ilkley Moor Baht 'at'. We used to do that. There was a high note and a low note. The fireman used to hold it back for the high and you pushed it forward for the low.

Fred Bateman

Fashions

J ust prior to the start of World War Two, Blackmore Fashions leased Fenny Stratford Town Hall to make paper patterns for the garment trade. They were the precursors of the many companies who evacuated premises in London. Tetley's and Rolex followed.

Donald Fraser Blane

Looking up the line from Winslow signal box towards Bletchley, *c.* 1952. The signalman is Dennis Comerford. (DC)

Changed the Rules

In 1938 they changed the rules for call boys. No-one under eighteen was allowed to leave the depot late at night. So we had to do a job called 'barboy' – a very dirty job. You had to get into the locomotive fireboxes to change the fire bars when they came in at night. It meant we had to stay in the depot. I didn't feel too good about that but the next stage was cleaner and by eighteen I had been passed as a cleaner for firing duties. When war began there were urgent requirements for footplatemen. The age limit for firing duties was lowered from eighteen years to seventeen. The first twelve months was supposed to cover shunting duties, but if you shaped up you were soon out and about. I passed for firing in August 1940.

Fred Bateman

The Rest was Up to Me!

One night going to sign the book at Bletchley No. 4 Box, I found a young lady working there. She had been sent up to Bletchley from South Wales under Essential Works orders. She also told me that she was living next door but one to where I was living with my parents. The rest was up to me! We have been happily married now for nearly fifty-three years, having brought into the world another generation of railwaymen.

Fred Bateman

Burlesque Theatre

John Blunt's butcher's was pulled down in 1876 and Fenny Stratford Town Hall built on the site. I think that was before Fenny was part of the Urban District. There was a stage in the Town Hall and it was on the circuit of repertory companies and burlesque theatre groups. Soon after I started work with Fenny Stratford Gas Light and Coke Company, I was sent to the Town Hall to deliver some mantles and clear glass globes for the footlights.

Donald Fraser Blane

Just a Dribble

I was fifteen years as a steam engine fireman before I passed for driving aged thirty-five. In those days it was almost a ritual to stop for water on the branch to Winslow, however much you'd got on. Your mate would nip across to the Station Inn. You'd turn the water on and then back about half a turn so it was just a dribble. If you were up on the tender pulling a bit of coal down, you'd give the signalman a few knobs of coal, or they'd ask what you were playing at, how long they could book you here. So you'd give him about a hundredweight and a half to keep him quiet. Then, when the tank was filled up to overflowing you'd slip the bag out, give a couple on the whistle and your mate would come running across wiping the froth from his mouth. There was a few noted for that. It was a saying that the railways ran on beer. They've clamped down now.

Fred Bateman

90

Main Artery

In the first part of the century Fenny Stratford was more important than Bletchley, with many more active businesses. The A5, Watling Street, was the main artery between London and the north. There were at least six public houses on the High Street – the King's Head, the Bridge Inn, the Bull and Butcher, the Swan Hotel, the Crown and the Three Tuns which all suffered after the M1 was built. With less through traffic Fenny declined and Bletchley took the lead. The gas office moved from Fenny High Street to 83 Bletchley Road (Queensway), premises vacated by Still's Grammar School.

Donald Fraser Blane

Leafy Lanes and the Old Fair

We had a police station at Fenny Stratford. There was not an awful lot of crime. Even though there were fewer cars you could be fined for riding your bike without lights. We used to ride all around the leafy lanes of South Bucks. There aren't many of them left, so much is built up. We had the best of it, something the younger generation will never know. Before the war we had all the excitement of the old fair with the big steam engines pulling the wagons and running the generators. They've gone. We used to swim down the Mill Pond. That's all overgrown now. It seemed huge.

Martin Blane

Milton Keynes has arrived and the funfair lives on. (RC)

Girls

When war broke out, girls took over the brick presses. They were as good as men once they got used to it. There were some young boys there, only fourteen. Girls might find a brick not pressed as hard as it should be, pick a bit off and flick it. Their hands would be going in and out under the presses all the while. By the end of the day you could hardly lift a brick. Those green (unbaked) bricks were heavy.

Bubbles Field

An Old Stager

Tommy Reid was an old stager with his own ways of doing things. Those were not right for the London Brick Company who took over Bletchley works in 1926. Ted Hersee was brought in as Tommy's assistant and almost immediately became manager. By that time, Tommy was walking with a stick and had to go. My job was sales and despatch. They kept on brickmaking until 1941 when stocks ran so high they closed production. Kilns were used to store ammunition.

Jim White

The Last Brickworks Chimney

When they blew up the last brickworks chimney one Sunday morning in December 1993 all that was left was a great big cloud of dust blowing up Beechcroft Road.

Reg Knapp

View from the top of the last Bletchley brickworks chimney ever built, 1964. The Saints Estate is visible in the distance. (RK)

Bletchley Park. Gwen and Martin Blane are in the foreground. (RC)

Christian Pacifist

When the war came in 1939 I had no intention of going into the army. I was a Christian Pacifist. I had to go through the mill of being called up and then go through a tribunal. I thought that would finish my newspaper. If I had gone in the army it would have. But I got a complete exemption on the grounds of the work I was doing. We lost very little circulation. I got the odd nasty letter, but very few, probably because my family was well known in the town. There was a shortage of newsprint. It was worse just after the war when we were down from sixteen or twenty pages to eight.

Bletchley was teeming with evacuees. A bomb fell on Bletchley Park and the people there tried to throw me out when I tried to report. I'd got a press pass and was officially appointed by the Home Office as the editor in charge of the district newspaper in the event of an emergency.

Ron Staniford

I Knew the Lady

I had learned shorthand and typing at Wolverton Commercial College. When I was eighteen I had to report to the Labour Exchange because I was old enough to be conscripted for essential war work. I knew the lady. She said, 'The Foreign Office want typists. It's local.' The women's services were full at the time. The lady made a phone call and my fate was sealed. At the end of the call she said, 'Oh, yes, they're interested in you. You go to Bletchley station on a certain train, Monday morning, where you will be met.'

We arrived at these very large gates. There was a guard with a rifle and bayonet, a guard dog at his side. We were taken to a little room where we had a lecture on the work we would do – serious war work. We were not under any circumstances to tell anyone outside about it. This was Bletchley Park.

Gwen Blane (née Brocklehurst)

Holiday Camp

We locals used to think Bletchley Park was like a holiday camp. We didn't realize what was going on there. We used to see people, they were billeted out.

Martin Blane

Strange People

The boffins of Bletchley Park were very strange. There were always a lot of strange-looking people wandering about, drifting in a sort of dream world of their own. There was one gentleman, he always had a mac and battered old trilby on his head, thick pebble glasses and he always carried a walking stick but he never put it to the ground. He carried it by the crook handle. Most people would swing a walking stick as they went along, or hold it like a cane. He walked with a shuffling walk. But we got so used to seeing him we just used to say, 'Oh, here's our funny man,' and that was it. You saw a few strange people like that. They were absorbed in their work, puzzling things out, trying to solve problems.

Gwen Blane

Reserved Occupation

I'd been on the Electric Light Company before the war and was put on a reserved occupation when conflict started, being needed to cover Bletchley Park. If the supply went off at Bletchley Park, it didn't matter where you were or what you were doing, you had to get it back on. That's why I never went into the Forces. I wasn't told. We didn't know why it was important. Over 1,000 worked there. They used to transport the shifts in camouflaged buses. They all worked in little shifts doing part of the job. Very few knew the whole picture which was about breaking German codes, using the famous Enigma machines and the giant Colossus computer.

Baden Powell

Very Nice People

They commandeered accommodation round about. In Simpson there were four next door to us, two men and two women. They were educated people: one was a Cambridge don, another a solicitor. Very nice people. Insley, the don, called me in to have a drink with him but they never mentioned their work. Miss Matthews had Bentley Bridgewater, director of the British Museum. After the war he'd come back on the train, bring his bike, a high two-cross-bar type. He'd lay it on the fence and come in for a chat. He had no airs or graces.

Baden Powell

Loco 46125, *Third Carabinier*, arrives at Bletchley with the Merseyside Express, 11 April 1963. (BB)

Patterned Socks

Then there was the writer Angus Wilson. He lodged with the mother-in-law, Emily Hall, next to Simpson post office. He had a little squeaky voice and liked brightly patterned socks. He was educated but hadn't got a clue about everyday, ordinary, common things.

Baden Powell

Outside the Gates

They built a hostel outside the gates for civilian girls. There wasn't room for everyone. The locals never knew who these strange people were and were rather suspicious. All their boys had gone off to war and were fighting. What were this queer lot doing in Bletchley Park? Skiving?

Gwen Blane

Gone to Ground

When I was with 26 OTU at RAF Little Horwood, some of us went to a dance at Bletchley Park organized by the Wrens there. They were short of male partners so they got in touch with the sergeants' and airmen's mess for any stray bods who might be available. We managed to find sufficient to fill a thirty-two-seater Dennis coach and a crew bus. I volunteered to act as one of the drivers. How I wished later that I had not been so silly. After the dance was over it was very difficult to find enough airmen and aircrew to go back to base with! They had all gone to ground for the night.

John Gillett

They Had Me As Well

All the evacuees came down on a train from Willesden. We were

95

shepherded along Bletchley Road to Leon school. It was early evening and we slept the night on rough straw palliasses. The next day we were all seated round the hall and local people came to pick us up for billets. I was down with two older sisters. This particular lady only wanted two evacuees. My sister said to her, 'If he can't come, you can't have us.' So they had me as well. They were lovely people. My older sister Maureen came to see us. A young lad was drowning in the lake off Denbigh Road. She dived in and saved him. The story made the national papers.

Evacuees only did half days at school. One week it was mornings, the next was afternoons. They didn't have enough room in Bletchley Road school to have us all day. The hall was sectioned off to make more classrooms. I liked having Thursday afternoons off because we could watch the cattle being sold and give the farmers a hand driving them to Bletchley station where they were loaded into wagons. I'd never seen cattle before in my life. We never had holidays back in London.

John Le Jeune

Elmers Grammar School

My time at Elmers Grammar School was very pleasant. When the war came it was taken over by Bletchley Park. Our main classroom had a direct hit from a bomb. After the war it became part of the teachers' training college.

Margaret Hollis

Chicken Feed

Eggs were scarce during the war. We got them from the grocer. Chicken feed was scarce. If you had a few chickens of your own you could forfeit your egg ration and have so much chicken feed. A lot did. Vegetable peel could be made into mash for the pigs. The allotment was important. We never knew what it was like to go without shallots or onions. My mother used to do up a parcel at Christmas for the old folk down the road. Poor old souls struggled to make ends meet.

They fed us well at Bletchley Park. The only time we had to talk was on the way to the canteen. We were never nosy towards each other. There was one little cockney girl, a dumpy little thing. When we came on shift she'd say, 'Oh, hello, back again?' I said 'Yes. How are you?' 'Brahned orf' was always the reply. Then she'd burst into peals of laughter. 'Surely you're not?' I said. 'Course I am,' she said. 'I shall be glad when this flippin' thing's finished and I can get back to a normal life.' I said, 'I think that applies to all of us.'

Bletchley Park was the first place I had venison. It was braised and I didn't understand why it was so pink. I thought, 'My goodness, where are they getting venison from?' My mother was struggling on eightpennyworth of meat from the butcher, lamb or beef. You did well to get chicken. And here we were with venison, beautifully cooked with lots of vegetables.

On a night duty between two and three in the morning you went for dinner. I could never face it. I felt sick because my tummy wasn't ready for roast dinner. A girl next to me said,

'Aren't you going to eat that?' I said no, so she ate mine as well. At breakfast you had a choice and she had my kipper. However, one morning there was a thick slice of ham I couldn't resist so I wrapped it up and took it home for mum. She said, 'My goodness, where did you get this?' I said, 'That's my breakfast, but I didn't bring my kipper from yesterday.' She said, 'Oh, you should have done,' and we laughed. They realized they'd got to feed us to get the volume of work.

When we were on the day shift we had an hour for lunch. We went in four sittings to eat, you had to say which one you wanted. If you managed to get served and eat quickly you had time to nip down into Bletchley and do a little bit of shopping. There were some rather strange little shops down there. The Castle Wool Stores was one. She had a wonderful collection of darning wools and different yarns. They came in small skeins. Often it was mercerized cotton. If you bought enough skeins you could make something like a pair of gloves. One girl knitted herself a pair of knickers in mercerized cotton. I don't know how comfortable they were! But, you see, everything had to be bought with clothing coupons and they didn't go very far. This is where the girls in the services scored over us because their uniforms were provided for. They got everything replaced.

Gwen Blane

Passion Killers

Service girls may have got everything provided for them but their

The old tin shops near the Bletchley Road railway bridge, c. 1958. (KB)

regulation knickers were what we in the Forces called passion killers!

Martin Blane

The Bells of St Mary's

My first memory of attending church was to sit up in the belfry of St Mary's with my father, Arthur Crane. I also went with Joyce Sear, daughter of conductor Harry Sear. We had a splendid view of the church and I could see my mother in the choir. St Mary's always had an excellent band of bell ringers and beautiful peal of light bells. It was a sad time when during the war

St Mary's church, early 1920s. (MH)

the bells were silenced, only to be rung in case of an invasion. But happily in the spring of 1943, when danger of invasion was thought to be over, it was decided to allow ringing again. By that time I was in the ATS. However, being stationed not too far away, on the Sunday morning I was able to arrive at Bletchley just in time to hear the bells ring out. It was a wonderful moment. Everyone in the road stopped to listen. My thoughts went to the young men away in various war zones, who but for the war would be singing at St Mary's. I hoped they would soon be safely home again.

Margaret Hollis

Never Heard Before

There were girls at Bletchley Park from all parts of the country, girls whose lifestyle I'd never come across before in my country backwater. It certainly opened my eyes to the different ways of young girls, their attitudes to their parents. Some of them were married! I heard language I'd never heard before. I certainly couldn't imagine referring to my mother-in-law as 'an old cow' or 'old bat', But they did, you see. It was their way, but not my way at all, though I suppose it was mild by comparison with what we hear on radio and TV now. But they were nice girls – happy, cheerful and considerate towards each other. When someone was feeling rough they'd cover and make life easy for her.

Gwen Blane

Makeup

My father didn't approve of girls wearing lipstick. Makeup was in short supply. You didn't get proper lipstick, you got refills. I can remember the local chemist, when he got in a supply of something like lipstick, one of the girls said, 'The chemist has got "Tangi" lipsticks, Gwen. Will you come with me, he'll only let us have two. Whichever one I get, will you get the other colour?' So that was what we did. I remember he'd got red and orange. The same happened with face powder. Tiny pots used to come in tiny cardboard boxes and you'd put the pots in your compact. There'd only be a choice of two colours. Hard luck if you didn't like them! Even soap was rationed, so if you wanted to augment your ration it was useful to pick up a shaving stick. These worked well on men's collars, they'd help lift the grime and save on household soap. You had to be careful, all sorts of things were in short supply.

Gwen Blane

Under the Table

My father was a Gloucestershire man. During the First World War he moved to be stationed at Tyringham. He had to march right to Staple Hall Road Camp ready for going abroad. During the last war when they were bombing Coventry we used to sleep under the big table in the living room. You could tell German planes by their sound – whirr, whirr, whirr. When the Americans flew off on daylight raids they'd be like a flock of starlings going over. The sky was absolutely full. They'd go over in the morning and you'd see ours go out at dusk.

Muriel Cousins

Please, Mrs Porter!

During the war I worked as a porter at Great Linford station but I had to pack up when my husband came home. They weren't used to women working. They used to fetch me up to Newport Pagnell to sort out the station books. I rode on the engine which was quite an experience. I missed it when I packed up, though the hours were long. The train stood in the station while you checked the tickets.

I was going to take my little girl into Northampton one Saturday afternoon. I went home from work, picked up my decent handbag. When I got to Wolverton station I talked to one of the railway superintendents, Mr Joy. I got on a workmen's train at dinnertime. At the first stop, Castlethorpe, I thought, 'I haven't got my purse.' One of the workmen saw me looking and said, 'What's the matter?' I told him and he lent me a pound, though I'd never seen him before. I asked him how I should pay him back and he said, 'Give it to Archie Joy.' He'd seen me talking to him and thought I was his wife. You wouldn't get that now. I sent him a note and a little bit extra thanking him for

Staple Hall, Fenny Stratford, *c.* 1917. (MB)

his kindness.

Muriel Cousins

Children's Home

My husband, Bill, was brought up by Miss Jones in Newton Longville in the mid-1920s. She took in three boys. At fifteen, Bill went to work at the brickyard. Then the war came and he joined the Beds and Herts Regiment. They were captured at Singapore and he was put to work on the Burma Railway for three and a half years.

Midge Day

Prisoner of War

I worked with Bill Day at the brickworks and like him I was captured at the fall of Singapore. I'll never forget being a prisoner of war. The Korean guard said to us, 'Line up and punch the next man in the face as hard as you can.' I thought I'd be all right if I was first in line but I reckoned without the Korean guard who set the standard.

Bert Viccars

Peak's Clothing Factory

When I left school I worked at Peak's clothing factory in

Denbigh Road, making army coats from eight till six for 10s a week. It was thick, heavy material. I worked a sewing machine for two years.

Midge Day

Home Guard

When the Second World War started three of us went to the old Fenny Stratford police station to sign up for the Local Defence Volunteer force, LDV for short and often known as 'Look, Duck and Vanish'. Of course they were best known as the Home Guard. There was a cubby hole just inside the door. This big, old sergeant opened the flap and said, 'What do you want?' We told him we had to register our names. First one goes up and says 'Baden King', then the next one says 'Baden Bates', and then it's my turn. He says, red in the face, 'I suppose you're bloomin' Baden Powell?' 'Yes,' I said. But they never told us much about what was going on during the war. They took all the road signs down.

Baden Powell

Blitz

On reaching eighteen all young men had to attend Bedford barracks for a medical interview for the armed forces. The officer stated that our conscription would be deferred for a time in view of our occupation. When we were called up we'd have to join the Royal Engineers Railway Operating Division, no choice. Meantime we were to fit in two nights a week fire watching, for which we received 1s 6d a night. Later we had to join the Home Guard B Company. As the railway platoon we would have to patrol all the railway installations during the night – bridges, shunting yards, signal boxes etc. The winter of 1940-41 was a miserable period with blackout conditions prevailing. All locomotives were fitted with anti-glare sheets to prevent fireboxes being observed by enemy aircraft. These heavy plate and side covers made driving conditions very hot. But after being stopped at any signal box and given the message 'Air Raid Warning Red' all precautions had to be taken. During the London Blitz a lot of traffic was diverted along the Oxford-Cambridge branch line. Traffic became so heavy that Bletchley had to give up some main line work to cover. About fifty volunteer firemen and guards were moved in from other areas to assist, being housed in sleeping and dining coaches in the carriage sheds.

Fred Bateman

Winslow was about nine miles up the Oxford branch from Bletchley. They were busy days during the war. Troops were passing through and train-loads of tanks were a common sight. I kept a sharp eye for suspicious characters. One memory is of a pair of Canadians chasing a couple of girls who were not keen on their acquaintance. They must have been drunk when they took a short cut between the couplings of a parked train just as the engine was pulling them tight. Lucky they weren't squashed!

Harold McLernon was one of my

Sergeant Baden Powell and members of his Bletchley Home Guard platoon. (BP)

colleagues. He worked the Bletchley boxes. He was an ex-sergeant with the Royal Corps of Signals and brought his army training to the signal box. He thought nothing of a twelve-hour shift starting at five in the morning and was always there five minutes early. He thrived on rules and regulations.

Dennis Comerford

In Short Trousers

When war came I volunteered for fire-watching, walking around to see if people's windows were blacked out. I wore a pair of my husband's trousers which I'd shortened. He'd been called up for active service and was surprised they didn't fit when he came home. He came home often before he

went overseas, hitch-hiking or cycling. Army pay was only 10s a week so I still had to work at the local Co-op. We had ration books for most food and clothing. It all sounds so drab fifty-three years later, but we made our own fun and I think we are better off for it these days.

Gwen Akins

Everybody Wanted It

I was on Newton Longville Parish Council for a while. Before the war, commoners didn't use the common – it was all ant hills, blackberry bushes, hawthorn bushes. During the war the 'War Ag' spent thousands of pounds clearing it and making it productive. It was very good land. After the war the commoners wanted it, so there was a problem deciding who qualified as a commoner. One rule was that if you had built your house in a day and had smoke coming out of your chimney, you qualified. The other was owning so many head of cattle or sheep. Before the war, only pheasants, blackberries and poachers used it. Afterwards they all wanted it.

Jack Blane

Awful Driver!

The loading dock foreman at the brickyard was Cyril Flexney. He had no mechanical knowledge. He said to me, 'You're a bloody awful driver,' and he said he was going to take me off. I said, 'That's your prerogative, Mr Flexney, but we must agree to differ.' I was a young bloke just out of the RAF where I'd been a senior NCO. I couldn't care less. I'd been one of the first to use a fork-lift truck to draw bricks from Bletchley kilns, on twelve-hour shifts. After two years I was effectively on two weeks' notice, relegated to hand-loading lorries on the dock. The transport manager, Chris Johnson, came down and asked what I was playing at. He said, 'Can you drive an eight-wheeler?' He fixed me up for a test in an old AEC Monarch, up to the Red Lion in Newton Longville and back. Flexney was furious. George Forbes, one of nature's gentlemen, said he saw no problem, so I became a driver.

Jack Bromfield

More Choice

After the war there was much more choice of jobs. There wasn't much call for shoe repairers and I wanted something different. When I got back to Bletchley I saw many changes. Some friends had got married, one had been killed in the Tank Regiment. The cycling group wasn't there any more. We tried to start another one but it never took off. The crowd and the fun we had was in the past. We were on a different plateau. We picked up life again where we could. It was a different life and world. Mother was pleased to see me back. Another four of my six brothers were in the services. My brother Jack was one of the first to be called up in the Royal Army Medical Corps. He was in the thick of it right to the end. It's remarkable he came out more or less unscathed. He was in Dunkirk, North Africa, Sicily, even D-Day.

Martin Blane

Alive and Well

When VE Day came we didn't really feel like celebrating in my family because my eldest brother was a prisoner in the Far East. He was taken at the fall of Singapore and the last we heard was a printed card with various bits crossed out: 'I'm unwell' was crossed out, leaving 'I am well' and so on. The first sign he was all right came through my sister-in-law's brother who was an officer in the REME. An RAF pilot contacted him with a message saying my brother was alive and well and would be

Bletchley brickworks in around 1949, with Jack Bromfield on one of the first fork lift trucks to draw bricks from kilns there. (JB)

on his way home as soon as he could.

Gwen Blane

The Future

The war was coming to an end and we started planning for the future. A chappie called Karl Moser came into the picture. He had been a reporter on the *North Bucks Times*. He came from Banbury to Bletchley before the war, taking over the *North Bucks Times* as sole reporter. He had to go into the Forces and was taken prisoner of war in the Far East. We were in touch and became very good friends. We'd covered stories together before the war, travelling in the same car and getting snowed up in Winslow. Anyway, we decided before Karl was released to send

him an invitation to join us and take over the editorship of the *Gazette*. He accepted, continuing after we sold it. We sold out to Home Counties Newspapers, they were building up their group. They held onto it for many years. We sold in the mid-1950s and had other interests.

We'd branched out into wholesale stationers in conjunction with our growing printing business. Eventually I started the *National Boys' Brigade Magazine*. The first edition sold 56,000 copies. I ran it until I retired around twenty years later. The printers were eventually taken over by Robert Maxwell.

I knew Robert Maxwell quite well. While I was editor of the *Gazette*, although I was a socialist I could not publicly come out politically. When I left that, I was free to join the Labour

Horse power helps political power on the election trail for the Labour candidate, Aiden Crawley, in 1950. (RL)

Party. I was Aiden Crawley's agent in the 1951 election. He changed sides, but he was a very good chap. I remember tearing round all the villages with him. In those days we had meetings, meetings, meetings in the villages. We used to fit four or five in one evening, with two supplementary speakers as well as Maxwell. We used to take them round by car. The candidate would start about six-thirty, speak for about twenty minutes with questions, and dash to the next meeting.

I remember taking Aiden Crawley round the villages. In those days the constituency was pretty massive, including Buckingham and west of the county, Steeple Claydon, all that area. To me it was a matter of principle. I didn't agree with everything. It's the same today, they're getting too right-wing. But my political principle was really a religious principle. I can't see any merit of any kind in capitalism. It results in the few making money on the backs of the many. The statistics today show it. Only a capitalist economy could have a national lottery for the purpose of making millionaires. I remember upsetting a Labour Party meeting. They used to run a sweepstake; members sold tickets every week. The chairman said, 'You'll take some, Ron?' I said no and gave him a little lecture when he asked me why not!

Ron Staniford

New Broom

Maxwell was to be a new broom when he came round the engine sheds during the 1960s. He wanted to know what was going on, but nothing came of it.

Fred Bateman

Youngest Manager

I managed Swanbourne village Co-op from October 1954 to October 1962. I was the youngest branch manager in Bletchley District Co-op Society and the whole UK. Being able to travel on my Matchless Twin motorbike helped my prospects. Few were willing to travel then.

Roy Stockham

Do What You Like!

All the farms have gone. It was lovely to have a farm at the top of the garden in Beechcroft Road. We used to go out blackberry picking. I went up the garden one day and saw Farmer Ramsay over the hedge. I said, 'Would you mind if I cut it down a bit?' He said, 'You can do what you like. I've sold the field for building.' That was quite a blow. The new houses changed things. We had anemones in the garden. I went up one day and they'd gone. A mum had told her kids to take them!

Reg Knapp

Robert Maxwell came here standing for Parliament. He came up the garden. I gave him five minutes.

Olive Knapp

Lucky We Were Young

I remember canvassing on a farm, trying to pay a courtesy call on the owner of a farm in the area. Hardly had we entered the farmyard than the farmer set his dogs on us and started chasing us with his pitchfork, yelling 'Git out!'. We were truly lucky and young enough in those days to be able to escape by sprinting out of the farmyard back to our car, just avoiding being attacked by his vicious hounds.

Mrs Robert Maxwell

In a Cage

There was a pet shop among the wooden shops under the railway bridge. The owner's son had a stall on the market. He had a parrot in a cage. It wasn't for sale. There were about four shops by the bridge. To us that was Bletchley. We used to get the bus down. There were only three a day. You had ten to fifteen minutes if you wanted to collect a prescription from Rushden's the chemist.

Reg Knapp

Roy Stockham, manager of the Swanbourne Co-op, in 1954. He was the youngest manager in the Bletchley District Co-operative Society.

Met His Wife

My brother worked for the Post Office. He rode a motorbike from Winslow before the war and met his future wife, Ivy, in those little shops near the station. She sold him his tobacco. He got transferred to Margate. That was good because it gave us somewhere cheap for holidays.

William Cripps

Train Robbery

I remember the train robbery back in 1963. The first I heard of it was when I went to work at the Post Office and there were a lot of police about. It happened not far away, at Cheddington Bridge – they faked a red signal. There was also the time in the late 1960s.

Inspector George Eames came rushing round saying 'Quick, quick! Ring the police: there's a bomb.' He had this parcel and it was ticking. Eventually we undid the parcel in the parcel office. It was a toy!

Cyril Freeman

Voice

There was only one doctor's near us, Dr Gleave. He'd been in the Forces and it affected his voice.

Olive Knapp

The Studio Cinema

I watched them building the Studio Cinema in 1937 and I saw it pulled

Bletchley Market after the move to the new site at the top of Queensway. (RC)

down. There's no cinema at all now.

Reg Knapp

The last time I went to the cinema was with my two daughters to see Elvis Presley in *Blue Hawaii*.

Olive Knapp

A Policeman

We were one of the few to have a car. One night a policeman knocked at the door. He said, 'Where's your parking light?' I said, 'We don't have one.' He said, 'You must have one!' But we don't see police these days.

Reg Knapp

Watercress

There was some lovely watercress by the tank at Winslow Station. Any crews stopping there used to nip over the fence, down to the stream and cup their hands full of watercress. You don't see watercress now. Winslow station gardens were lovely, as they were at Verney.

Fred Bateman

Ferrets

I was a permanent way man working mainly on the Bletchley-Buckingham branch. I remember going to Swanbourne station. They had ferrets to catch the rabbits there. Rabbits were a nuisance, burrowing under the tracks and causing them to go up and down. If

Swanbourne sidings, 1963. A mixed goods train is ready to depart for East Anglia. (DB)

you couldn't catch them they'd send the rabbit man from Northampton to gas them. I went off eating rabbits when I saw one with myxomatosis. It had white foam inside. Letting that disease loose took away a workman's cheap meal. Wild flowers! We used to take bets on how many heads you could find on a cowslip. I found a double-stalked one with thirty-two on, but they wouldn't have that. Bee orchids in June and July were a rare sight. They're just like bumble bees with pink petals around, looks like a bee going into a flower. Railway banks were a nesting area for partridges, ducks' nests and a lot of other birds. When you were working it was so peaceful with the cuckoo singing in the background. I liked seeing all the birds and animals. You couldn't beat what we saw along the branch line – lovely scenery. We've destroyed such a lot. They've ruined the railways. We're paying through the nose to repair the roads.

You worked forty-five or fifty years for your gold watch in my day. I missed the railway because we helped each other. Mates wouldn't see you struggling. When I went into the factory I was just an individual standing behind a bench all day and getting pins and needles in my feet for twenty-four years.

Des Tunks

Gold Watch

Dad went up to London to get his gold watch when he retired from his years as a guard and looking after Swanbourne sidings. He said he appreciated it but would much prefer to have the one he'd used during his working life. They were supposed to give them in but they let him have it. He handed it in and it came back embossed. He received the gold one as well.

Gwen Akins

Freed

Freed from editing the local paper, it wasn't long before I was elected to the Bletchley Urban District Council during the early stages of town development. I followed my colleague Harold Price. They were adventurous years. We used to sit up as late as one o'clock in the morning tackling the problems of development. One of the biggest problems was matching the number of houses to the growing population. There was also a need for more industry.

Ron Staniford

Street Parties

I came to Bletchley in 1945. On VE Day they told me to come over and take pictures. We had all the street parties organized by Alf Long. I snapped him and the rest. That must have gone on for two or three days, then I dashed back on the train to Brackley, coming back with the photographs in a couple of days. I was the *Gazette's* wonderful new photographer. I knew hardly anything. We bought some new equipment. The first darkroom we ever had was down in Aylesbury Street behind Percy King's shop. Percy King was a keen naturalist and his garden was a keen naturalist's garden: absolutely overgrown!

Our darkroom was a tumbledown old room. It had some stairs. I suppose it was a cottage one time. It was cold and damp, not ideal for a dark room or printing. I remember the first winter, 1946-47, was one of the hardest in living memory. The place was completely frozen. We had water everywhere. That didn't do my spirits much good. Then Bletchley printers built new premises by what was then the Central Gardens and opposite the Co-op where they sold the cream buns which we lived on.

Ray Lubbock

New Town Development

Bletchley was turned down in the original Abercrombie plan and put up a plan to expand to 60,000. But no town of 7,000 had the finance needed for quick development which would have to include new water and sewage works, roads and housing estates etc. Tremendous capital was needed, way beyond a small council. The Ministry wrote the New Town Development Act drafted by a Labour government in the early 1950s and it was finally approved by the Conservative government in 1952. The whole development was undertaken by the whole council – it was never a party matter. The Conservative Party leader W.H. Johnson was one of the most enthusiastic people. The planning authority, not the Council, had to decide on the layout and size of estates. Everything had to be tied together. You couldn't afford the housing supply to get ahead of demand because they were a charge on the rates, but if you allowed the reverse and people came pouring into town on the promise of a house there would be trouble. That was the worst problem.

Ron Staniford

Ray Lubbock's assistant at work in the *Bletchley Gazette* darkroom. (RL)

News Photography

The equipment I used for news photography was primitive. I went down to London and bought myself a press camera which I didn't know how to use. Looking back, it was the world's worst choice. In those days you used flash bulbs filled with something like silver paper from chocolates, aluminium foil. They usually went off, but not always. I went round with this camera to functions. I started doing football, which I knew little about. It must have been in that cold winter, 1946-47, I was photographing a darts competition at a pub in Fenny. Maybe it was in the Rose and Crown. I went in from the freezing cold to a humid bar and the whole camera dripped water. After that the camera shutter wouldn't work properly for a long time. One of the things I did in a big way was the Bletchley Show in the Leon Rec on Bank Holiday Monday. I used to go around doing all the stalls and all the people. I remember the editor, Karl Moser, on Bank Holiday Monday when Bletchley bridge was flooded. I was sent out to photograph various people or a car creeping through the water.

Ray Lubbock

Looking for a Job

When I came up from London I looked around for a job and got one at Tetley Tea's packing factory for six months. Then I found there was a wholesale greengrocer's, V.B.A. Stevens,

A wartime military convoy in Aylesbury Street, Fenny Stratford. (GL)

in Buckingham Road. They sold out to Green's who used to own the cattle market field where they built Sainsbury's.

John Le Jeune

I remember Vern Stevens when he was an errand boy on a bicycle at the little greengrocer's they called Covent Garden, near the station.

Margaret Hollis

Fenny Neglected

They started developing in 1951. Woolworth's was put up, Fenny was neglected. We bought our house in Beechcroft Road in 1946. I biked to work in Fenny, all weathers, twice or three times a day. In those days I used to go home to lunch. It was 2.6 miles from the shop. You could bike straight through the middle of Bletchley in those days. Going up Freeman's Hill you weren't obstructed by cars but by cyclists. There seemed to be hundreds but you hardly see them now.

I remember the Development Corporation in the early days coming round to us in Aylesbury Street with lovely pictures, coloured roofs and all that. Fenny was going to be all gardens and trees. Fenny never recovered, though it seems brighter than Queensway with a lower percentage of boarded-up shops.

Ray Lubbock

Fire damage to the premises of Bletchley Printers and Central Garage, late 1940s. (RL)

Out of Steam

When the steam sheds closed, everybody got new noms de plume. Instead of being a loco foreman arranging rosters, three of us had to go over to the new diesel depot to do the traction arranging in conjunction with the controller. The regular foremen had to go onto No. 8 Platform and become station supervisors – roster clerks, more or less. All those young men who'd been firemen waiting to pass for driving were offered £320 to go. Most of them went down to Barclays Bank. My son did thirty years in their printing department after he was made redundant from the railway.

Fred Bateman

A Good Friend!

All went well at our newspaper printing works until a certain gentleman, who was notorious and a good friend of mine, did some arson jobs. One of his targets was my darkroom in 1948. My wife was pregnant at the time with our first child. The first two years' negatives were lost. Then Bletchley Printers bought new premises at Fenny and set up the *Gazette* branch office. There I did the photographs. It was all going nicely until two years later. I was told we had sold out to Home Counties Newspapers and that was the end of my activity in that line. I went on to build up my employer's photographic business and camera shop in 1949. This carried on for ten or twelve years, then they sold the retail business to a chap in London

113

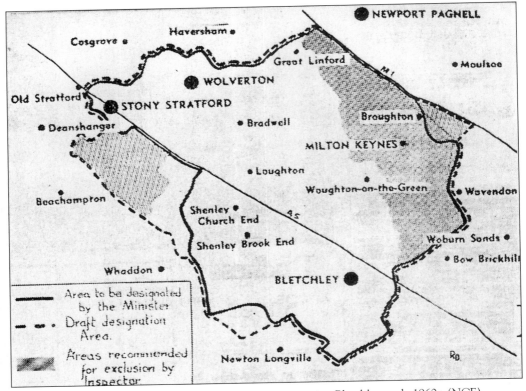

A map of the proposed new city of Milton Keynes, encompassing Bletchley, early 1960s. (NCE)

and I cut my links with Bletchley Printers. I was on my tiny tod!

Ray Lubbock

A Day Out

When I was growing up in the fifties you had to go to Aylesbury for a hospital and that was a day out. Lucky nothing ever happened to me that was urgent. Our doctor was Dr Gleave. He had a croaky voice. If you walked into his surgery he knew who you were straight away. They don't know you from Adam nowadays unless they've got notes. Dr Gleave's waiting room was a ramshackle place. Seats were things like an old settee he'd thrown out of his house or a row of old benches to sit on. It was first come, first served. He was a lovely doctor. His surgery was in Bletchley Road.

Jenny Stacey

Making Plans

The town surveyor, John Smith, became the town manager and he spent time interviewing, trying to get factories down. We didn't want people and no jobs. Eventually we pulled through. This was all before Fred Pooley and the big county plan for the new city of Milton Keynes. Much of the credit for expanding Bletchley goes to Arthur Bates, John Smith's predecessor, who spent most of the war making plans and specifications so that when the OK came for local authorities to start building we were there, we'd have the plans and the land. We started off in the Water Eaton, Manor Farm, Pinewood Drive area – the fields where we used to play as kids. That all went first. Then it was gradually down to Water Eaton. All that area was filled in. Then we had an interesting development.

There was a housing shortage during Macmillan's era and the Home Office asked us to build an estate of what were called steel houses. These were basically steel with brick facing. We accepted this as long as we could put our people in. That's the Whiteley Crescent off Newton Road.

Then back at the other end, London councils were putting the pressure on. They planned the Lakes Estate. You find Bletchley Council being blamed quite wrongly for that estate. We had an agreement that a percentage of Londoners would occupy them. We built them and nominated a percentage from our housing list. We had a lot of criticism about that estate, justifiably. The flat roofs were soon leaking water. You would have thought London County Council architects would have known better. It was a habit then. From 1950 to 1960 that was the way, and not one school roof didn't leak.

Ron Staniford

Bletchley station's Pilot shunting engine with driver Reggie Felce and fireman Chris Kelly. (CS)

Call the Fire Brigade!

I came to Bletchley in the early 1960s. My friend Frank McIntyre had already transferred down from the London Fire Brigade and I decided to come too. When you came down the A5 from London, Bletchley was a place on the left-hand side. You saw the Beacon brush factory, that's where Beacon Retail Park is now. Bletchley had two brush factories; the other was in Victoria Road. That was quite a large area with Nissen huts. They used to make good quality brushes and cheaper ones. They were just starting to build Bilton Road, I think. We came down to a very fluid situation. I had two children aged about eight and ten at the time. I

Bletchley's horse-drawn steam fire pump at work at Shenley around 1920. (RL)

couldn't see any future for them in London. We got a secure home up here, a house of our own, not just a room. I was on the Ealing housing list for twelve years before that.

Frank Hutchinson

A Place to Live

I came to Bletchley because I wanted a place to live. You couldn't afford a place in London in those days. I joined the London Fire Brigade after time on the railways mending wagons. I saw somebody get a £50 retirement presentation – a pound for every year of service. I decided then that I wanted a job with a pension and joined the brigade. They were looking for blokes to come up here and I volunteered. I was

blooming happy to be here. I got a nice house.

London was the best place to learn the job but I never regretted coming up here. We came up to do the day shift at Church Street; the part-timers did the nights. They lost money. Church Street was a funny little place but we knew they were building a new station at Sherwood Drive. We watched it going up. It cost £110,000 and opened in 1965.

Frank Hutchinson

Go Back to London, Where You Came From!

When I went back to London after the war and got married, I lived

Another load of bricks comes onto the road at the main gates in Newton Road, October 1964. The elm trees were lost to Dutch elm disease in 1975. (RK)

over my father's greengrocer's shop in Earls Court. I knew we'd never afford a house so I said to my wife, 'You know I was evacuated to Bletchley during the war. Let's go up there and see if there is any property.' We saw the plan of the houses, liked them and put down a deposit. When it was ready we moved in. When we first came up I didn't have a job. I went to the Labour Exchange to see if they'd fix me up. The conversation went: 'Are you skilled?' 'No.' 'Are you semi-skilled?' 'No.' 'Well, you might as well pack up and go back to London where you came from.'

John Le Jeune

Records

All brick delivery records were broken from the fifties to the seventies. The brick industry flourished and the new estates grew up. Sir Malcolm Stewart came every Christmas to hand the office staff their bonus personally.

Reg Knapp

Class Differences

I was quite friendly with the Frasers, vets, who lived in a big house three or four doors up from the doctor's, opposite the school. I used to go to school with their daughter, Sheila. They had two sons. My gran cleaned for them. They had moved up to the big house that's now the Registry Office. They had birthday parties in the back garden. That's gone now. There were definitely class differences. My nan brought up five children on her own. It was a case of any work she could do, she did. She did a lot of cleaning for the higher class folk of the district. Some people did look down on others but it was fading out as I grew up.

Jenny Stacey

Opportunity Arose

I was working as a draughtsman in Post Office Telephones at Norwich and was promoted to leading draughtsman. Opportunity arose for me to come to Bletchley Park. I'd always wanted to go into teaching and this was one way because they had a training school. I knew nothing at all about Bletchley except what I'd read in the paper, that there were these proposals to develop the old brick clay pits, flood them and import some sand to make an inland holiday resort. It sounded a great idea – lakes with sand and holiday chalets. This was September 1964. We came down to look for suitable properties. There seemed to be nothing going. I remember looking at a Wimpey estate they were building and the only trouble was people were camping out overnight waiting for them to release each home. They released about three or four at a time, but you never knew when the next ones were coming on and of course there'd be a big increase in price.

Dennis Sizeland

118

Expensive

When we first came to Bletchley we stayed with my wife's aunt and uncle, Harold Price. We wanted a home of our own, so we looked around and nearly bought a house opposite the Studio cinema. But we thought £1,000 was a bit expensive in 1945. Harold Price had a house offered him which was £50 less so we belted up to see it one night. We weren't married at the time but we thought it was just the job. When we came up to Beechcroft Road it was a cold, damp night and the people had put the gas fire on in the bedroom so it was all nice and cosy. We learned later that it must have been on for hours to make it that warm and cosy!

Ray Lubbock

I Thought We'd Never Get There

As firemen we had different sorts of shouts up in London. Obviously we never had field fires. But Bucks firemen could learn a lot from our way of doing things. We helped each other. When you go to a fire or accident you don't think about the horror, you thought about what you could do. We saw some terrible accidents on the M1 when it first opened. We used to ride out on a pre-war, open-topped engine nicknamed Elizabeth because of its number plate, EBH820. It was a good old appliance, with crash gearbox but it had overdrive. In London we had to reach a scene within minutes. Up here we had to use maps at first and it took so long sometimes I thought we'd never get

Bill Billings' dinosaur sculpture looks as if it is rampaging through the grounds of Leon School on the Lakes Estate, Drayton Road. (RC)

there!

Frank Hutchinson

I Liked Bletchley

I liked Bletchley before all the changes. When I came up from London in 1962 it was a little market town. There was a lot of nice countryside. Now a lot of the streams run through pipes underground.

John Clarke

Crime

I don't like the way Milton Keynes has developed – it's ideal for crime. I liked the open countryside. But we couldn't

argue with it because it's the only way we'd have got the opportunity in the London Fire Brigade to transfer up here. I've only been back to London once, just after we moved up. My wife was homesick. When we got there everything looked so dirty. We never wanted to go back after that.

Frank Hutchinson

No Job for a Lady

I don't think the fire brigade is a job for women. They're not made for it. Men aren't really. It's hard enough for them. If a woman was in charge of me I wouldn't like it but I'd accept it. But you always get someone who'll make your life difficult, pick on someone because they're a woman, for example.

John Clarke, a 1960s newcomer, on his 1927 replica farm traction engine, enjoying the still abundant countryside along Buckingham Road. (RC)

The same thing happens with blacks. It's the way some people are. Being in the Forces during the war probably hardened us up. Maybe we'd be like it anyway. I've no time for all this therapy and counselling they do today. Where would all these people be if they'd had to face what I've had to? A lot of people make jobs from being do-gooders. They walk about as if they're saints.

Frank McIntyre

All in One Street

A little group of criminals did come down together from London (Islington) and were put all in one street. They created some problems. But the Lakes Estate was for 7,000 people. That's the size the town used to be. The problems have been exaggerated. People moved into the estate; it didn't take long to build. The problem was a considerable shortage of building material and there were pressures to push as many as possible into as small a space as possible. Space was decided by central government, so many square feet per family.

Ron Staniford

North Bucks for Labour

Harold Price used to run a Sunday night gang including three Methodist ministers. In 1945 there was an election. I had quite a long time interviewing and photographing Aiden Crawley. He took North Bucks for Labour. I went to Buckingham where the count took place and remember photographing Churchill going through in a car. I was up on the balcony photographing the winners and was confused about which election was which. I remember photographing Clement Attlee in Wolverton market place. When they started expanding Bletchley it was the famous Mr Bevan and Mr Morrison and other big names in front of my lens. I remember Aiden Crawley changed from Labour to Tory.

Ray Lubbock

Dropped the Glass Negatives

My sister got married a year after us. When you went out to photograph a wedding you'd take a big camera that took big five by four plates and a roll film camera that did the other stuff. When my sister got married my assistant dropped all the big glass negatives. Fortunately they'd been proofed, but they said 'Proofs' all over in aniline dye. I didn't know then that you could get rid of aniline stains with Stanner's Chloride, but where do you get that today? Fortunately we had some pictures on roll and we could copy some. Colour came in during the early sixties; then, at weddings I would repeat the main groups in colour and offer them as extras. But few wanted them.

Cameras were heavy and had to stand on heavy wooden tripods and at first I did all the work travelling on my push bike. Imagine going to a wedding with a big black box on your shoulder and a great big tripod behind. I remember going over to my first wedding at Woburn by bike. In the middle of

Woburn there's the church of St Michael. I went there and found no wedding. Someone said, 'Oh, the church is up there,' so I went off puffing away. We made it. I remember doing five weddings in one day.

When I took on the shop in 1949 starting in retail cameras, the first colour films were coming in. The first one popularly available was Dufay colour, using dyes. The film was printed all over using a microscopic pattern of colours. You photographed through the film and the colours reacted in various positions. You processed the film by reverse, turning positives into negatives, held it up to the light, and there was your picture.

Ray Lubbock

Church

My wife taught in Bletchley and at first we travelled in from Brackley where we'd met at the Methodist church. It was a good rail service from Brackley to Bletchley – there was a personal service on the railway then. Uncle Harold Price was a Methodist. When we came to Bletchley we started working in the Sunday School in Bletchley Road, where they were short of teachers. We had a tandem in those days which we'd bought to go on holidays and we rode down on Sundays to the church. It was a good church in those days, with a good choir. My wife is very musical. Till our second child arrived in 1950, we tandemed down regularly. Then we moved up to uncle's church, the Freeman Memorial. Those were the days of strong church youth

P.J. Baker's photography shop in Aylesbury Street, *c.* 1920. (EL)

clubs. There had been a youth club in the Albert Street premises at the back of the Co-op and they had a very strong youth club down in Bletchley Road, Queensway, in the hut at the back. That's since been burned out. The Albert Street premises were sold to the Co-op. Then the youth club came up to Freeman's and was the life and soul of the party. It was led by a chappie who was clerk at the County Court, Stuart Robinson. He was affectionately known as Robbie. After fifty years it's time I found some successors, but it's quite difficult to get people to take responsibility.

Ray Lubbock

Time for Promotion

I worked in Bletchley Park at the drawing office training school from 1964 to 1968. The I thought it was time for promotion. I'd run the course for tracers, just tracing information onto maps, and for drawing office assistants. I'd repeated these for about four years and thought it was time I got into real teaching. I went to the teacher training school, also in Bletchley Park. I went in as a mature student, doing two years' training, studying maths and art. They were enjoyable years and I qualified in 1970.

At Bletchley Park, in the days when I was there, the wartime buildings were much as they had been. There was still a lot of secrecy about what had gone on on the site. Our HQ was in the mansion and we used it for social purposes in the evening. It was the first place I ever heard any stereo broadcasting, because one of the post office engineers there was very keen on radio and that. In the evenings he'd set up speakers and we heard stereo broadcasts for the first

Methodist dignitaries view the church being built, mid-1950s. Dr Pauline Webb of the Methodist Missionary Society, a broadcaster and World Church Council delegate, is on the left and Harold Price is at the extreme right. (RL)

time.

Dennis Sizeland

A New Ball Game

All the first diesel drivers were old steam drivers. By thirty-eight, I was deputy loco foreman. You weren't the regular foreman and if you didn't make it you were taken off the panel. It was like probation. That was 1954. It was 1965 when I got a regular job down the depot as traction arranger. Then I went to Watford as inspector. Then the area manager took it all over and I became traffic manager at Watford. This was a new ball game, going out at weekends and dropping signals on, being in charge of rail operations. These blokes used to come by on the engines and say, 'It's

warmer up here.' They pulled your leg.

When you take your interviews and go to see the superintendent, he'll tell you straight you've got no friends. The set answer is, 'I've got all the friends I want at home.'

Two of us ended up as area controllers, Arthur Jinks and myself. Signalmen in the box resented a loco man like me coming into the box as area controller, but our basic training put us in good stead. Area controllers, many thought, had to be ex-signalmen, but not necessarily. I had to learn all the rules and regulations and be able to handle the box. We had periodical examinations.

When you were traffic manager you'd just leave a signal box number. They didn't expect you to be behind the door all night, so long as they knew where to contact you. We used to walk up

Fred Bateman on his last day of driving duties, in electric loco uniform in 1965. He was photographed by his fireman, Wally Lee. (FB)

Aylesbury Street when they slung us out of the pub! There'd be policemen in there having a drink. You'd come along and see people saying goodnight to each other. But now all sorts of things happen in Aylesbury Street. Blooming windows get broken left, right and centre. That was a pastime a few years ago in Aylesbury Street.

Fred Bateman

A Bit of a Rebel

I was chairman of the Juvenile Court and a bit of a rebel. I've got a great deal of faith in young people and have been dealing with them through the Boys' Brigade all my life. I was quite certain I could sit a young criminal in a chair before me and spend an evening with him. That's the answer. I think that if a lad knows that someone is interested in him, his family and what he's doing and what his problems are, you've got a good chance of sorting him out. Colleagues used to pull my leg, but the police thought it was great.

A good many lads have come to court and I've said, 'What have you to say for yourself?' Nothing. And many magistrates go on and pass sentence and that's that. I had a different technique. If a lad was wearing a Manchester United badge, for example, my first question would be, 'How's United getting on these days?' And then get him talking about football, ask him if he played, find out about his interest. Then, having got him talking, I'd switch and say, 'Well, this is a silly thing you've been doing. Why do you do that?' Then he'd tell you. That technique always worked, but I wouldn't call it soft.

One tries to apply a punishment that's fair to the victim as well. The chairman of the bench has to convince the offender it's fair, then he will accept it. It was a difficult job, but I enjoyed it. Community service was a good idea. I remember one middle-aged chap who'd stolen a lot from his employer. We gave him a long term of community service working with handicapped children. I saw him some months afterwards and he said, 'I've got through the sentence but I'm carrying on with it.' That was a success. I don't think anyone is born evil; environment is the main thing. A

The face of change at the Motor Show in the new city centre. (RC)

lot depends on the parents' attitudes. I wouldn't like being a parent – they have to hold a balance between being too severe and too easy. Many are too easy, for instance the mother that comes into the juvenile court, which wasn't uncommon, and weeps, saying, 'I don't know why my Jimmy's turned out like this, I've always given him everything he's wanted.' Well, that's the reason.

My parents went to church. I always had friends in the church, the Baptists at Water Eaton. When I was a boy, Free Church, Anglicans and Catholics were beyond the Pale. Fear of the unknown was the problem. Catholics held services in Latin, in Church Street. I had a good Catholic friend on the council. I remember when the Civic Service was in the Catholic church and we had to have another priest to translate. Nowadays you could sit in a Catholic church and it could be a Baptist or

anything.

Ron Staniford

A First-Class Job

Apart from a few practical mistakes the Development Corporation have done a first-class job.

When Milton Keynes took over from Bletchley Urban District Council we decided to celebrate the end of the old council with a pageant. We got hold of Dougie Loak who'd done a lot to push the cause of the theatre in North Bucks. We said, 'Dougie, we want to have a pageant to celebrate and we want you to write it.' He said yes, and did a tremendous job. He dived into all the history books picking out every scrap about Bletchley and pulled it all together. Dorian Williams produced it

125

Aylesbury Street on a sunny day in the early 1930s. (GL)

and it ran for a week in the sports hall in the Leisure Centre. Then on the last day, 31 March 1974, there were hundreds performing. Like the rest of the week, the hall was packed. The crowd came out about half past ten and went over to Leon Recreation Ground for a firework display. Then they all went up to the council offices, took down the old Urban District flag, then raised the new flag of Milton Keynes. The Boys' Brigade sounded the Last Post and Reveille. It was fantastic.

When I got home an angry person in Whaddon Way, a mile away, telephoned to complain that the bugle had awoken her little boy. That was officially the end of Bletchley. I wasn't sad. I was very proud of Bletchley but it was closing to make way for something greater. Things don't stay the same.

Ron Staniford

Roundabouts

The biggest mistake was how Milton Keynes was first developed. I said at the time flat tarred roofs were a bad idea. Milton Keynes also affected Bletchley shops – the local Woolworth's soon went. But the impact of Milton Keynes on Bletchley is hard to judge. It's probably one of the best road systems in the country. You need extra front wheel tyre pressures for all the roundabouts. In the early days the developers worked with too many untried ideas.

Roy Stockham

A Bit of a Nuisance

In the old days the hunt used to meet. We used to go down to Water Eaton

Baden Powell and Muriel Cousins, Simpson Village, 1994. (RC)

to see them off on their journey. The hounds would go around and pick up everything they could, including everyone's food and my chips! Those days it was quite something, we didn't object. It was more about enjoying the sight of them in their red coats. As time went by they just became a bit of a nuisance, looking as if they thought they were better than anyone else.

Jenny Stacey

Different

They're doing a lot of work to improve the road to Buckingham. When I used to cycle out there from Bletchley on summer evenings the gully was lit up by glow worms. The light was an eerie green. Little did I think that it would remain in my memory so long.

Ray Akins

Pride and Joy

The green on which the war memorial stands was in the days of my childhood the pride and joy of Mr Healy. The grass and border were always in perfect condition. On Armistice Sunday evening with the bells ringing half muffled, the robed choir each with a gas flare torch walked from the church to the green, to be joined by the British Legion and the civic bodies for a short service at the memorial. Afterwards a church service was held, the church always being very full. It's nice to see the memorial still well cared for today.

Margaret Hollis

Complaints

When we were at school they ruled us with a rod of iron. These days

127

dig. We didn't find anything for some time. Eventually there were only four of us left digging. I went up one day and said, 'Any luck?' No, they said. I said, 'What's that you're standing on?' It was a leg bone. Charlie Peacock from our brickworks canteen was in charge. We found two headless skeletons and three more with heads. I also got involved with a dig down Watling Street, at the Roman camp Magiovintium. They found all sorts of things. Some stuff went to Oxford museums. A skull's photo used to hang in our office with the message: 'As you are now so too once was I. As I am now so soon will you be.' I wrote underneath: 'I've been waiting 1,000 years for resurrection and I'm still waiting.' Upstone, the office manager, roared.

Reg Knapp

Sun Shines on Bletchley

I had good lodgings with Jim and Doris Read back in the thirties. To me the sun was always shining on Bletchley because I met my wife Gwen there. I go there now and I feel feelings I don't get anywhere else.

Ray Akins

A family gathering at the War Memorial on St Mary's church green, late 1920s. (MH)

you daren't make a move without somebody wanting to complain and these complaints are getting carried. There's doubt about the future of the multi-storey car park, with so much car crime. And the caterpillar at the Leisure Centre – there's doubt about maintaining that.

Fred Bateman

Magiovintium

Price's field in Newton Longville had a mound. We thought there must be something under it. Some of us started a